America's Back Roads and Byways

America's Back Roads
and Byways

BY RON FISHER

PHOTOGRAPHS BY SARAH LEEN

NATIONAL GEOGRAPHIC

WASHINGTON, D.C.

CONTENTS

PAGE ONE: *Bonneted Kentuckians Mona and Mina Thevenin and Lola Howard retrace part of the Oregon Trail in Nebraska.*
PRECEDING PAGES: *In Michigan, lowering February skies heighten the allure of an icy byway skirting Lake Superior.*
OPPOSITE: *About to be judged queen at a festival in Pine Prairie, Louisiana, Samantha Guillory readies her smile.*

ROADS OF CONTENTION

Grand Staircase-
Escalante

Like a sinuous byway, the Escalante River meanders through the eastern part of the largest national monument outside of Alaska. The proclamation creating the monument calls it "the last place in the continental United States to be mapped."

PRECEDING PAGES: *Rugged and remote, the Grand Staircase-Escalante National Monument wrinkles south-central Utah. Highway 12, paved only in 1971, runs across its northern edge, from tiny Escalante to even smaller Boulder.*

S AY YOU'RE A WRITER and you're exploring Grand Staircase-Escalante National Monument in southern Utah. You're going to be haunted by one word: "indescribable." The landscape is so huge, so dramatic, so many-hued, so difficult, and so remote that words—at least the words I know—are not up to the task. Others have tried. Geologist Clarence Dutton, who was here with Col. John Wesley Powell in 1872, wrote, "It is a maze of cliffs and terraces lined off with stratification, of crumbling buttes, red and white domes, rock platforms gashed with profound cañons, burning plains barren even of sage—all glowing with color and flooded with blazing sunlight."

In his classic *Desert Solitaire*, Edward Abbey took a stab at it. Floating down the Colorado River through these canyons with a friend, he wrote,

"The sandstone walls rise higher than ever before, a thousand, two thousand feet above the water, rounding off on top as half-domes and capitols, golden and glowing in the sunlight, a deep radiant red in the shade. Beyond those mighty forms we catch occasional glimpses of eroded remnants—tapering spires, balanced rocks on pillars, mushroom rocks, rocks shaped like hamburgers, rocks like piles of melted pies, arches, bridges, potholes, grottoes, all the infinite variety of hill and hole and hollow to which sandstone lends itself...."

It's through just such a landscape that I drive down a dusty, bumpy byway called the Cottonwood Canyon Road, southward into the heart of the new national monument. It's a 46-mile-long graded dirt-and-gravel road that is passable in dry weather only. It follows the Cockscomb, a major buckling of the Earth's crust that divides the Grand Staircase from the adjacent Kaiparowits Plateau. I'm on a short pilgrimage of sorts, headed for Grosvenor Arch, a rare double arch named for NATIONAL GEOGRAPHIC magazine's first full-time editor. Cattle range the fenceless countryside; a calf stares at me and wags its tail as I drive by. Piñon jays, a delicate turquoise, fly alongside my car.

At the arch, black-throated sparrows trill from the bushes, and cliff swallows soar at arch-top level, which is as tall as an apartment building. Ravens caw from somewhere in the distance. I can hear a gust of breeze coming from a mile away; it's chilly as it sweeps across me, even though the day is bright and sunny. A string of half-a-dozen cows sets off down the middle of the road in a purposeful manner; maybe they're going somewhere for a drink. Of other human beings, there are none.

It's the sort of place you can come upon when you explore the back roads and byways of America, which is why I'm in Utah. We have chosen half-a-dozen regions around the country to explore—regions that are widely scattered, geographically diverse, yet each still containing something of its historic culture. In addition to Utah, we'll visit the snowbelt—northern Minnesota and Wisconsin and Michigan's Upper Peninsula; the steamy Cajun country of Louisiana; the Olympic Peninsula at the far northwestern corner of the country; the Cumberland Plateau in the heart of Appalachia; and the lonely vistas of western Nebraska.

Two Franciscan priests, Father Francisco Atanasio Domínguez and Father Silvestre Vélez de Escalante, passed near this part of Utah in 1776, seeking an overland route from Sante Fe to Monterey in California, spreading the faith among the Indians along the way. They left no evidence of themselves except the name Escalante, now attached to a town, a river, and the country's newest national monument. Until September 18, 1996, the 1,880,400 acres that now make up the monument were

Teeth of the Cockscomb rise alongside Cottonwood Canyon Road, one of several two-lane tracks that crisscross the nearly two-million-acre national monument, created in 1996.

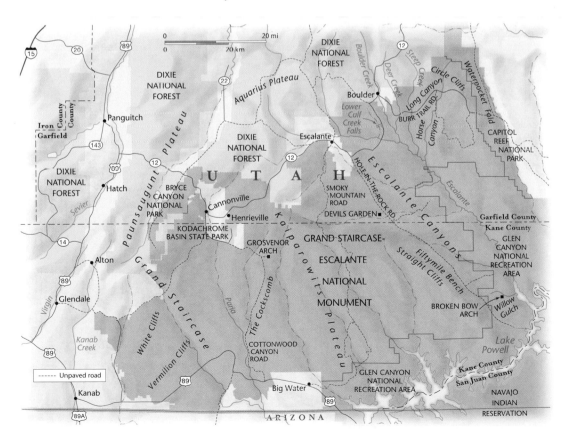

Early morning fog rises over Kodachrome Basin, a region of red-and-tan sandstone spires left standing when surrounding Entrada Formation eroded away. The name was proposed by National Geographic Society visitors to honor the pioneering brand of color film.

PRECEDING PAGES: *Mindee Brindley and David Munson dance at their Junior Prom. Escalante High School's 125 students attend classes from 8:00 to 3:45 Monday through Thursday, then devote Fridays and Saturdays to extracurricular activities, some of which may require day-long bus trips.*

---

just a huge tract of land managed by the BLM—the Bureau of Land Management—for grazing, mining, and recreation. But on that day, President Clinton signed a proclamation creating the monument. Delaware could fit comfortably within its boundaries. Its elevation ranges from 4,100 feet to 8,300, from low desert shrub to grassy steppe, from sage and piñon-juniper woodlands to ponderosa pine at higher elevations. There may be as many as 100,000 archaeological sites within the monument. The "staircase" is a series of terraces and cliffs piling up north of the Grand Canyon; you'd have to walk 40 miles and climb more than 5,000 feet of elevation to ascend them.

The language of the proclamation is unusually lyrical for government prose: "This high, rugged, and remote region," it says, "where bold plateaus and multi-hued cliffs run for distances that defy human perspective, was the last place in the continental United States to be mapped." It's the first national monument to be managed by the BLM, and the agency is struggling to find a balance among all the conflicting interests that want a part of the monument. Like a giant, color-splashed Navajo blanket, the monument is having its corners tugged in different directions by different people. There are ranchers and Mormons, who generally feel that new restrictions on land use will interfere with their traditional livelihoods; environmentalists who feel the restrictions don't go far enough; government bureaucrats trying to satisfy as many people as possible and offend as few; civic leaders and businessmen with one eye cast on a rapidly growing tourist industry.

Feelings can run high. There have been shouting matches at public meetings, threats and counterthreats, vandalism, and tears. The draft of the BLM's management plan was an inch-and-three-quarters thick.

A small, hand lettered sign in one of the restaurants in the little town of Escalante says, "There's not much to see in a small town, but what you hear usually makes up for it."

As I make my way in and out of the monument on those dusty little byways, I make it my business to check in with as many of those interested parties as I can, and I listen to what they say. I get an earful.

CRAIG "SAGE" SORENSON HAS worked for the BLM for 25 years, lately as an outdoor recreation planner. "When I was a kid I liked to go hiking in the hills, and one day my brother told me I smelled like sage. The name stuck." We talk in his office at the BLM headquarters in Escalante. "Yes, having the area designated a national monument is bringing change to the local community, but that change was on its way. Visitation was rising. A lot of people who want solitude and remoteness were beginning to find Escalante.

"I've been involved in management here for some time now, and I can tell you that the people planning the monument truly have the concerns and welfare of the local community in mind."

Escalante sits astride Utah Highway 12, often called one of the ten or so most scenic drives in the country. It passes through slickrock canyons, red rock cliffs, and pine and aspen forests. The town's quiet Main Street is as wide as a French boulevard and is lined with a bank, the post office, an outfitter or two, an under-stocked and dusty supermarket, a gas station with a mini-mart attached. Videos are available at the supermarket. You can buy a T-shirt that reads, "Don't Worry, Be Hopi." There are no newspapers or magazines to be found and no wine or beer in most restaurants, only nonalcoholic Coors, a nod to the Mormons. Escalante is the second largest town in Garfield County, a county that has not a single traffic light.

Beyond Escalante, Highway 12 winds north through expanses of slick-rock country, including the Escalante Canyons, and gingerly threads a narrow ridge where steep cliffs on either side of the highway fall hundreds of feet. The section of highway from Escalante to Boulder wasn't fully paved until 1971; Boulder claims that it was the last town in the U.S. to have mule-train mail delivery. In the restaurant of the comfortable and unobtrusive Boulder Mountain Lodge, I have breakfast with owner Mark Austin, a man with a keen interest in the area's burgeoning tourist industry.

As waitresses come and go, offering fresh coffee, Mark says, "With the paving of the road, it was obvious tourism was going to increase. One of the big chains had plans to build a motel here, and I thought maybe I could do it better, build a place that was aesthetically compatible with the little cow town that Boulder used to be. We built it in 1994.

"The monument was created in 1996, and it was a necessary move. The quality of the area was already undergoing a gradual erosion.

"I've lived in southern Utah for 26 years but am still considered something of an outsider. I can sympathize with the old-timers. Emotionally, the land is theirs. The Mormons have a long history of persecution, and many of them think it's happening again. They think the U.S. came in and took this land away from the state of Utah and is forcing this national monument on them. Many are still stuck in an old mind-set: We'll make our living by digging it out of the land. They don't see the incompatibility of an oil field or a coal mine and air quality. They say they don't want things to change, yet they wanted paved roads. But they're not dealing with reality. I try to tell them, you have to start making some hard choices or someone else is going to make them for you.

"The land management issues here are as complex as the landscape, and the local culture in a way is as harsh as the landscape. I'm in a lawsuit with the town now, trying to get a restaurant liquor license. Many of the locals are bitterly opposed to that.

"So far, I'd give the BLM a B-plus. It's the first time they've tried to manage a national monument, and they're being pretty creative.

"But it comes down to roads. Roads provide the access that inevitably brings development and encroachment. The county, caught up in states' rights, wants the right to build roads wherever they want *(continued on page 23)*

(continued on page 23)

Making the rocks resound, a Buddhist monk from India checks the acoustics of a slot canyon. He and his brethren have visited the region four times over the last five years, raising awareness and money for the Buddhists of Tibet. They stay several days, hiking and horseback riding, as well as lecturing, singing, dancing, and chanting—and selling T-shirts and prayer flags. The singing in the canyon, according to one witness, was "magical."

Nature crafts bizarre shapes and forms in Devils Garden, an officially designated, 200-acre outstanding natural area within the monument. Entrada sandstone spires sprout alongside hoodoos, domes, passages, and small arches (above, left). One of the largest—Metate Arch (above, right)—echoes the smooth, concave shape of ancient Native American grindstones.

PRECEDING PAGES: *Stars wheel across a nighttime sky, made bright by a long moonlight exposure. Broken Bow Arch, in Willow Gulch, soars over boulders that fall as stress fractures and erosion gradually enlarge the span.*

them. The county's strategy is to create roads that will make an area ineligible for inclusion in the official wilderness system. And wilderness to these people is like Darth Vader."

A ROAD EVEN MORE BEAUTIFUL than Highway 12 departs Boulder a few yards from the lodge. After my breakfast with Mark, I take a leisurely but breathtaking drive along it. The Burr Trail Road is hard surface for its first 31 miles, to the border with Capitol Reef National Park, then turns to dirt and gravel. If it were paved inside the park it might be more crowded, but I have it virtually to myself. From Boulder, it crosses Deer Creek and The Gulch, then ascends up the length of Long Canyon through scenery that is truly stupendous. At the Circle Cliffs it circles toward Capitol Reef and the convoluted terrain of the Waterpocket Fold. You begin to understand why so many people are tussling over this landscape.

One of the prime jugglers in the tussle is Dr. Suzanne Winters, executive director of the Escalante Center. I find her in a cluttered makeshift office at the Escalante High School. "The Escalante Center," she tells me, "is a non-profit corporation, a consortium of players representing many of the interests in the area. Members of our board represent the Escalante High School, Garfield School District, Southern Utah University, Garfield County, the Utah Travel Council, the Last Wagon Museum, and the BLM."

The hope is to build an actual campus on grounds next to the high school and offer accredited classes, field camps, and research opportunities to students and scientists. "We want to help the BLM adhere to the science mandate of the presidential proclamation," she says. "It designates the monument primarily for science. The BLM is not a scientific or research organization, so we want to help them set up a science education and research program. We want to provide facilities for scientists and let our K-12 students work alongside them.

"We just had our first-year anniversary, and it's working pretty well, though politics are a problem here. Garfield County has traditionally operated as an adversary of the BLM. They've been in lawsuits for 20 years, over roads especially. There's an 1860s law that grants rights-of-way to the county on roads that go through federal lands. Garfield County wants to maintain those roads to their standards—which means in some cases rights-of-way 60 feet wide. The ranchers who live out there want them for getting back and

---

Perhaps one of the country's most spectacular drives, Utah Highway 12 threads a narrow pass north of Escalante. Tourism here has swelled since the monument's establishment, increasing between 1996 and 1998 from 520,000 to 850,000 a year.

forth. But the BLM's tendency is to maintain the travel surfaces as they are. That and proposed closure of more than a thousand miles of roads within the monument are the crux of the problem.

"I consider myself an environmentalist—though I've learned not to use the "E" word in Escalante—but since I've moved here I get really angry with people who don't understand the complexities of the issues, trying to tell people here what they can and cannot do. They don't understand. People in Escalante are living hand to mouth, they're struggling. They've struggled for a hundred years, but they chose to live here. And I think that's the key: They've chosen the struggle. They're very proud of that struggle. Unless you somehow accommodate these people, who are after all a part of the environment, in a balanced approach, then there's something wrong.

"I tell the locals, unless they start taking control and managing the growth, they're going to be overrun, because the people who are coming in have more experience and more money and are used to having things their way. And the local people aren't accustomed yet to dealing with tourists. I was in a restaurant the other day and overheard a couple—Germans, I think—ask for box lunches. The proprietor said, 'We're not doing lunches yet. It's only 9:30.'"

Escalante was settled in 1875 and named on July 4, 1876. Its Mormon settlers grew fruits and vegetables, black walnuts, and even mulberries for silk worms. The first homes were dugouts, then log houses. Irrigation ditches along every street provided water; animals were kept corralled each day until the clean water had been brought in. Phone lines reached the town in 1908, and a young blind man, Leander Shurtz, was put in charge of the switchboard. He manned it until 1945 and could recognize the voices of all the town's 1,200 residents.

From Escalante, I head for the Panorama Trail in Kodachrome Basin State Park—whose name was bestowed by the National Geographic Society in 1949, then changed to Chimney Rock in 1962 to avoid a lawsuit, then changed back again when Kodak recognized a good promotional opportunity. I feel like a walk, and the trail meanders for an easy three miles through colorful Entrada sandstone formations.

The day is clear and sunny, with a few puffy clouds and a comfortable temperature. The prickly pear is blossoming a delicate purple alongside the trail, and overhead I can hear the murmur and see the contrails of five separate jets, all at the same time. Unusual sedimentary pipes stand 30 to 50 feet in height and are composed of erosion-resistant coarse sand bonded together with calcite and feldspar. They've been given fanciful names—Fred Flintstone Spire, Ballerina Spire—and survive from distant geologic ages. I traverse a grassy flat studded with juniper, big sagebrush, rabbitbrush, and four-wing saltbush. The Hat Shop is a concentration of orange Entrada spires capped by sandstone slabs. The

Roundup brings rancher Todd Phillips onto the national monument. Cattle spend the winter grazing here, on leased land, then are moved in April to summer pastures in national forests.

FOLLOWING PAGES: *"Roundup is just about the best time of the year," says rancher Randy Gleave, relaxing at day's end with family and helpers. "Though it's a lot of hard work. You've got to make sure you've found all the new little calves and put them with the right mothers." Randy and his neighbors camp here for two weeks each year, rounding up and moving about a thousand cattle.*

trail skirts the foot of one of three huge slickrock domes, then curves around it and merges with an old coach road. At a signboard I turn upward and ascend to Panorama Point, the apex of a debris cone, via steep switchbacks. There, with a view of velvety grasslands and piñon-juniper woodlands, I have my lunch, an apple and a Snickers. The wind in the junipers murmurs softly, and I nearly doze in the warm sun.

AFTER THE BLM ISSUED ITS DRAFT management plan in November 1998, the public had some four months to comment on it. About 7,000 people chose to do so—this in Garfield and Kane Counties, whose combined population is about 10,000. The BLM laboriously categorized and catalogued and studied the comments, applied the ones they thought appropriate to their plan, and issued a proposed plan in July 1999.

The plan includes, it says, "a strong BLM-directed science program," and

places different parts of the monument in different categories, depending on the amount and kind of use they have received in the past. It provides for minor recreational facilities such as signs, pull-outs, and toilets in some areas but not others, for instance, and promotes scientific research.

And what sort of response are you getting to your proposed plan, I ask the BLM's monument manager, Jerry Meredith. "We feel like the plan is being received as well as can be expected," he tells me. "In a situation like this one, where there are numerous, diverse viewpoints, you can't expect complete acceptance or for everyone to embrace it. But we feel like things are going well, that most people understand that they have been heard."

Jerry emphasizes the BLM's responsibility to adhere to the President's proclamation and to manage the monument largely for science. "We have tried to limit the kinds of activities that we felt would potentially damage or alter natural systems before they could be studied. In just our first year we were involved in some way with more than 40 different scientific research programs in the monument, and others that we simply permitted.

"It's amazing what people are finding out there. Just last week a researcher found a new plant. We've found new populations of listed species that nobody knew existed. Dinosaur trackways have been found, and a hadrosaur, all in just the last few months. Remember that the exposed geology in the monument goes back 270 million years. There are very few places where you are able to look back across 270 million years of Earth's history."

The plan must go through what's called the protest period: If commentators feel their concerns were not treated appropriately in the final plan, they can protest over the heads of the local BLM people to the bureau director. Jerry expects there will be some protests.

And the ugly issue of roads within the monument continues to rear its head.

R OADS, ROADS, ROADS, WHO WOULD have thought that innocent back roads and byways could generate so much heat?

In the BLM's plan, any road that's been maintained regularly, even if only once every three or four years, is still open. If it was built with equipment and it's got culverts and is maintained with motor graders periodically, it is not being closed. But the monument has been explored for uranium, coal, oil, and gas for decades, so there are scores of little two-track routes that run out and dead-end in the middle of nowhere. Those are being closed by the BLM.

There are now almost 900 miles of roads and trails still open in the monument; environmentalists think that's far too many, and local ranchers think it's far too few. About 60 percent of the monument will be within approximately a mile and a half of a road of some sort.

Sunset falls on Hole-in-the-Rock Road, a dusty, 57-mile route blazed by Mormon pioneers in 1880. Intent on creating a road to Bluff on the San Juan River, they first had to carve a precipitous way through and down the cliffs along the Colorado River.

I ask rancher Billy Cox what sort of grade he gives the BLM. "A very low F," he says. "Many of us have been using those roads for years, often just in winter when our cattle are out there. We use 'em to check on the livestock, to maintain our water sources, to put salt out. But in rainy years, like this one, the roads grow up and these environmentalists, with their lack of experience, come in and look at an overgrown track and think it hasn't been used in a hundred years. Whereas maybe three months ago I used it three times.

"We think these roads were guaranteed to us by the U.S. government through the 1866 mining law. And Utah law says any road that's been used by the public for ten years is a public right-of-way. But the federal government is totally ignoring our rights and the rights of our state.

"I've sold my permit to run cattle on the monument. I'll ranch now just on my private property. I can't fight 'em anymore."

Nonetheless, Billy is a member of an organization called People for the USA, "a coalition of individuals, communities, industry, and local governments joined together to advocate common-sense reform of environmental regulations," according to its handout. "I will sign up for anything that will truly save our country," says Billy.

Makeshift marker (above) points the way in Willow Gulch. Few trails as such exist in the Escalante monument, where hikers must find their way along unmarked routes across slickrock and up twisting canyons. A hiker (opposite) has little chance of getting lost in the narrow confines of Spooky Gulch.

Gregory Aplet, a forest ecologist with the Wilderness Society in Denver, devoted a lot of time to advising and commenting on the BLM's management plan for the monument. "There were some really good BLM people on the planning team," he says. "And I like the direction they were going in and the changes they made between the draft plan and the proposed plan. But they didn't go far enough."

The Wilderness Society would like to have seen ATVs—all-terrain vehicles—banned from the monument entirely, for instance, calling them "noisy, dangerous, and destructive" and "totally inconsistent" with the monument. Even if restricted to roads, the Wilderness Society believes, ATVs will "bring mechanical noise in to shatter the sense of remoteness and unspoiled nature" that is the object of monument protection.

Greg says, "While it's true the BLM decreased the access of ATVs, the proposed plan increased the miles of roads open for ATVs. And with the increased attention the monument is getting, we can expect increased use of those roads. And that's where the problems will arise.

"The plan doesn't proscribe development in the monument, so it leaves a lot of room for mischief in the future. There's lots of wiggle room in some of the language, activities that are forbidden 'unless no other alternative exists,' for instance. In the future we may have a completely different administration in place, with different values, but this plan will remain the legal document guiding monument management." *(continued on page 36)*

Patterns and colors emerge from eons of erosion by wind, water, and scouring sand. Minerals tint Peekaboo Canyon (above, left); faux faces line a wall in Horse Canyon.

FOLLOWING PAGES: *The braided Paria River curls through the western part of the monument, a region of lusher tablelands. The Paria joins the Colorado at Lees Ferry.*

Greg wonders about the future of Escalante, in the face of tourism that's sure to increase dramatically. "Every time I go over there, I get the image of a huge wave that's about to crash down on the town."

Greg's colleague at the Wilderness Society, Pete Morton, a resource economist, sees things through the prism of dollars and cents. He points out that historically the economy of the American West was based on extracting and exporting the region's natural resources—agriculture, mining, and timber harvesting. But in the new American West, home of such "knowledge-based" service workers as computer programmers, engineers, and stockbrokers, amenity resources like scenic vistas, recreation opportunities, and wildlife are becoming more important features of the region's economy.

"People have a way of planning for the future by looking in the rearview mirror," he tells me. "We tend to think of the Escalante monument region as a big coal-mining area, but in fact in 1995 just 24 workers were employed in the mining industry in Kane and Garfield Counties. Same with ranching. Almost the entire monument is allocated to grazing, even though the proportion of total personal income provided by ranching dropped from 7 percent in 1969 to less than one half of one percent in 1996.

"And there's a huge anti-federal-government, states'-rights culture here, but between 20 and 30 percent of residents' total income is now provided by various federal sources: social security, pensions, subsidies, and payments. If you eliminated the federal government and gave all its responsibilities back to the states and the counties, the economy of those two counties would be devastated."

So I GO FOR ANOTHER WALK, THIS time with Grant Johnson, who, with his wife Sue Fearon, operates Escalante Canyon Outfitters. A former uranium miner, Grant is using his mining expertise to hollow out a boulder the size of a gymnasium, creating windows and rooms inside it, which will one day be his family's home.

He leads walking trips for tourists—horses carry the supplies, the people walk—of several days' duration into the canyons around Escalante. He talks earnestly and enthusiastically about geology, and tells me hair-raising stories of plunging through flash floods astride his horse. First the water is up to his waist, then over the horse's head, then over *his* head, then the horse is spinning in the flood and Grant is clinging to a bush. "It was the last crossing before home, and the horse knew it, so he was willing to try. If you give a horse his head he'll usually get through. Of course, if you let him have too much head he'll turn around and go home."

We walk one warm morning along the canyon walls abutting the Escalante River. Grant names the wildflowers we pass: the bright splash of the claret cup

Former uranium miner turned trail guide, Grant Johnson scrambles across slickrock in Willow Gulch. He and his wife, Sue Fearon, owners of Escalante Canyon Outfitters, lead horse-pack trips into the canyons along the Escalante River, stressing the geology, prehistory, and ecology of the area.

cactus; the sturdy cliffrose, a gnarled shrub thick with creamy pale-yellow flowers like wild roses; a low-growing shrub called Brigham tea, from which the early Mormons brewed the drink. I ask about wildlife in the canyons. "There are turkeys and gray fox and bobcats. The coyotes can be a problem. They eat our cats."

We descend to the river, which here is only about 20 feet wide and about a foot deep. Its banks are lined with willows, and the shade is cool and green. We find a clump of blue jay feathers on the trail, evidence of a hawk's kill. Grant points out more wildflowers: princess plume with tall golden racemes, and bright red scarlet buglers. "This is Russian olive," he says. "An exotic. It's really taking over."

Desert varnish paints a cliff face in Willow Gulch (opposite), where one of Grant Johnson's horses grazes. Above, Lower Calf Creek Falls tumbles from a 126-foot precipice, then disintegrates on moss-green boulders. The national monument, harsh and rugged yet fragile and beautiful, today suffers the tuggings of diverse interests—ranchers, government agencies, environmentalists, and proponents of tourism—as it seeks its future.

Grant finds evidence of early Native Americans—a sandstone grindstone for grinding seeds, remnants of ancient walls and roof marks against the cliff face, fire-pit stones, a fragment of pottery, ancient ash from a fire. A tiny lizard with part of its tail missing scurries across the trail.

Petroglyphs survive on the canyon walls: trapezoid bodies with narrow waists wearing antler headdresses, a figure holding a crude bow and arrow, turkey tracks, a bighorn sheep. And a remarkable image: We stand before a cliff face high above our heads that has 150 handprints painted on it, all in rows, "like a register of some sort," Grant says. It's like a billboard with one emphatic message: Stop.

And, as we stand there in silence, a canyon wren's silvery song falls upon us, a gradually slowing and descending series of liquid *tees* and *toos*, like a whistling waterfall.

My next stop, a thousand miles to the southeast, will have a different set of props: Instead of sere canyon walls, there will be live oaks dripping with Spanish moss; instead of BLM rangeland, bayous. I'm on my way to the Cajun country of Louisiana. ■

BAYOU BYWAYS

Cajun Country

Sur les pointes, a snowy egret dances in a lagoon on Avery Island, in the heart of Louisiana's Cajun country. Late in the 19th century, a few captive egrets were released from a rookery here; today some 20,000 of the graceful birds return to nest each year.

PRECEDING PAGES: *With a nugget of raw chicken, guide Ron "Black" Guidry tempts a 'gator to the side of his boat. He conducts tours in the swamp near the calm waters of Bayou Black, near Houma. Some 500,000 Cajuns live in Louisiana, descendants of exiles from Nova Scotia.*

SPRINGTIME IS JUST getting a good start when I land in Lafayette, Louisiana. The small city sits nearly dead center in a triangle composed of the 22 parishes, or counties, known as Acadiana, home to most of Louisiana's 500,000 Cajuns. They survive as an ethnic group, managing the delicate balancing act of remaining distinct and unique culturally while at the same time finding a comfortable fit in 20th-century America. The heart of their heartland is an eight-parish region composed of Lafayette Parish and seven adjoining parishes.

Uprooted from their homes in Nova Scotia at the start of the French and Indian War in the mid-18th century, many Acadians found a final home in southern Louisiana. Adapting well to the steamy bayous and lush prairies, they found their neighbors

shortening their name first to "'Cadiens," then to "Cajuns," which is how we know them today.

The back roads that thread their realm beckon with steamy allure—quiet black bayous, wind-rippled crawfish ponds, miles of sun-warmed prairie grasses nodding in soft ocean breezes. Cajun country divides into four distinct geographies: The fertile bayous built up along rivers; the coastal marshes, where the oil and gas deposits lure prospectors; inland swamps like the wild Atchafalaya Basin; and the prairies where rice, cattle, and soybeans season and mature.

Every little town has a kwik-stop of some sort and a couple of cafés. In them you can gorge yourself on lunchtime buffets that feature rice, gumbo, blackened catfish, red beans, and crawfish étouffée. And peach cobbler. After such a lunch I ordinarily find a shady spot—church parking lots are good places—for a nap.

South of Houma a narrow hard-surfaced highway runs straight toward the coast. Utility poles have a single skinny wire running between them. Fishermen are planted here and there on the banks of the bayou; you can mark their location by their parked pickups. Turkey buzzards soar overhead, and red-winged blackbirds chirp from roadside grasses.

Beyond Chauvin, a bayou runs alongside the road for mile after mile; it's lined with moored shrimp boats. The season hasn't begun yet, so they're at rest. Their butterfly nets hang from spars and look like Spanish moss. One of the boats—*Miss Brunella*—is for sale, and I fantasize for a moment. "Hmmm. Suppose I…."

Nearer the low-lying coast, most of the homes are up on stilts. At the end of the road there's a town named Cocodrie—Cajun French for "crocodile." Miles of marshes and bayous stretch to the horizon. Gangly shorebirds like ancient dinosaurs lift off from patches of still black water. Tiny work boats come and go in a busy sort of way, and distant vents emit orange flares of burning natural gas. Sunshine glitters on the ocean.

A group of Louisiana universities and colleges maintains a facility here, the Marine Consortium, which since 1979 has coordinated and stimulated the state's activities in marine research and education. It provides coastal laboratories to more than 20 Louisiana institutions and conducts research and educational programs in the marine sciences. Its 75,000-square-foot complex consists of labs, classrooms, offices, a library, and housing facilities for up to 92 people.

I wander through the museum area, where I learn that the salt- and freshwater marshes, the mudflats, the forested scrub, and the sea-grass beds of Louisiana's coast are being lost at an alarming rate; that Gulf coastal wetlands and barrier islands provide critical habitat for 75 percent of the migrating waterfowl traversing the U.S.; that during a 1988 beach cleanup along the Gulf

From a bridge on Burns Point Road, the Intracoastal Waterway takes aim at New Orleans, carrying barge and pleasure craft to points east.

FOLLOWING PAGES: *Landing less than a whopper, a dockside fisherman at Cocodrie shows off his catch. Here, at the ball of the Louisiana boot, Highway 56 ends abruptly at the Gulf of Mexico.*

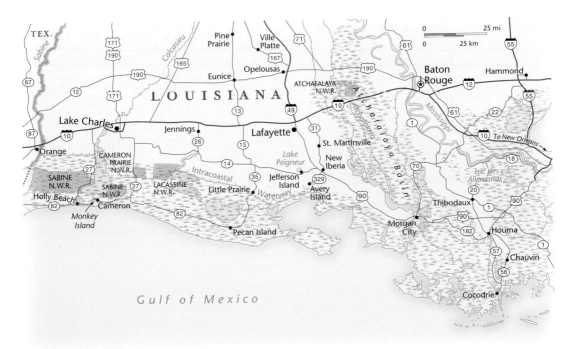

Coast more than a million pounds of trash and debris were picked up and that 68 percent of it was plastic; that those plastic yokes from beverage six-packs may persist in a marine environment for 450 years.

THE ARRIVAL OF OIL-AND-GAS exploration brought big changes to the Cajuns and to their culture in the 1930s. It also ended their isolation. Ron "Black" Guidry remembers an early schoolteacher from Texas, who came with her husband who worked in the oil industry. "She'd whip the hell out of you if she caught you talkin' French," he says. "Now they're bringing in teachers from Quebec to teach the kids how to speak French again!"

Black and his little Catahoula dog Gatorbait take tourists in a flat-bottomed, canopied boat into the swamps near Houma. He can carry 49 at a time, and his running commentary is given first in English, then in French. The day I join him, half the crowd is from France, for Cajun country is a popular destination for French tourists.

In a calm and stately manner, we depart from Black's dock on a branch of the Intracoastal Waterway. He explains about Gatorbait: "I drag her along behind the boat to attract alligators. Used to use my wife, but I lost her a couple of times and now she won't do it anymore." Even when translated, the French are not sure what to make of this and look askance at one another. Duckweed covers quiet backwaters, and water hyacinth is thick. Alligators doze in the sun, some small, some eight or ten feet long. Nutrias graze the shore like woodchucks. "Some of you may have heard of the nutria, the big rat they make NutraSweet out of," says Black. Purple gallinules tiptoe among the water hyacinths, and bald eagles and great horned owls perch in dead trees. A great blue heron glides by overhead.

"Growing up, we were aware that we were poor, barefoot people," Black tells me, when we talk later. "My daddy was a truck farmer. He grew vegetables and took them to the French market in New Orleans, so I grew up working on the farm. As kids, we were laughed at and joked about because of the way we spoke. But five years in the Army taught me to lose most of my Cajun accent. We spoke both French and English as kids. When mama wanted to talk to daddy about something she didn't want us to know about, she spoke French, so as a result, we learned French."

Sunset ignites troubled coastal waters: Large canals for navigation and smaller ones that give access to oil rigs bring salt water ever farther inland along the Louisiana coast, degrading rich wildlife habitat where Cajuns traditionally hunted and fished. Flooding that once enriched wetlands with silt has been largely stopped by riverside levees.

*Folk art fills a Chauvin backyard. Here, toward the southern boundary of Cajun country,
shrimp and oyster boats line Bayou Terrebonne—and eccentric neighbors cause little stir.*

Black spent some time with the 101st Airborne Division, then was with
the Louisiana State Police, then was in the ready-mix concrete business, then
was a professional musician touring with a band. He runs our craft up against
a bank, gets out his tiny Cajun accordion, and plays and sings a couple of
songs, including "Jambalaya." Gatorbait, tail wagging, takes center stage, faces
the audience, and sings along. She looks deliriously happy.

Black's accordion was made for him a few years ago. "It's called a ten-
button diatonic accordion," he told us. "It's a German instrument. But during
World War II, the Cajun people couldn't get parts from Germany, so they took
things from around the house to build their instruments. The cedar in mine is
from an old chifforobe that I had. The buttons are chrome-plated .44-caliber
bullet caps, and the connecting rods are aluminum welding rods. The keys are
one-inch, half-round molding from around the house, with reflector tape on
them. The knobs are regular little cabinet knobs. The return spring inside is a
big baby diaper pin, and the strap is a man's belt. The only things brought from

a factory are the bellows and the reeds, which still come from Germany and Italy." Once or twice, as we troll along, alligators that recognize Black's boat come swimming slowly toward us, their knobby snouts and eyebrows visible above the still water. Black dangles chunks of chicken for them, which drives Gatorbait frantic with excitement. "She's a round-up dog," says Black. "She thinks she can get out there and round 'em up."

W̲ITH BLACK'S ACCORDION ON MY mind, I drive to the town of Eunice to visit with Marc Savoy, who makes Cajun accordions, in addition to maintaining a successful career as a musician. "A Cajun accordion is essentially a harmonica that you play with your fingers," he says, as we sit in his workshop behind the store where he sells musical instruments, yet another sideline. "You get one tone if you push, another tone if you pull.

"When the Acadians moved here from Nova Scotia the accordion hadn't been invented yet. They brought with them a complex, intricate fiddle music. But when the German immigrants arrived—and it was they who brought not only the rice but also the accordions—the music changed a lot. The accordion has only seven notes, so you can only play simple tunes. Before accordions, we had mazurkas, polkas, contra-dances, jigs, square dances—all kinds of fancy dance steps. But when the accordion came, everything disappeared except the waltz and the two-step.

"Cajun kids absorb the music. They learn the music first, then learn to play an instrument. Cajun music is easy, but it's not simple. I can teach you to play "Mary Had a Little Lamb" in five minutes, but if you want to play it Cajun style, that'll take you a lifetime of studying and listening.

"It's high energy music, good for dancing."

I have an opportunity to see for myself that Saturday night. The Liberty Center for the Performing Arts in Eunice hosts a live radio show—the "Rendezvous des Cajuns"—each Saturday night. The host, Barry Jean Ancelet, conducts the proceedings mostly in Cajun French but partly in English and partly in a mishmash of both. It's a charming old theater, I find, with paintings of plump, scantily clad ladies on the walls, a dark maroon curtain, and movie theater seats.

The first act is the Creole Zydeco Farmers, a five-man band made up of two guitars, an accordion, drums, and a sort of washboard. Zydeco has been described as "a musical merger of such sounds as rhythm and blues, jazz, rock and roll, gospel, and Cajun music." The MC joshes with the band in a curiously accentless French— he sounds like an American speaking French with a flat midwestern twang. There's a reference to the band's *"nouveau CD."* A clearing in front of the stage is immediately crowded with dancers. *(continued on page 56)*

Fearsome denizens of Louisiana swamps, alligators—until a few years ago
listed as an endangered species—now multiply so prolifically they supply souvenir shops,
where tourists purchase their grisly remains (opposite).

FOLLOWING PAGES: *Spanish moss and cypress knees catch the fading afternoon light*
over Lac des Allemands, a popular fishing town northeast of Houma.

The band plays "You Won't Miss the Water 'til the Well Runs Dry."

Next comes a Cajun stand-up comedian, A. J. Smith, who performs in English. He tells stories about his cousin Loveless, who combines careers in veterinary medicine with taxidermy. "His motto is either way, you get your dog back."

A local musician, Horace Trahan and his band, the Ossun Express, close out the show. Horace plays the accordion. He's young and nervous and very serious at first but gradually warms up, then whoops and hollers. He speaks English with a French accent. Their music is infectious and irresistible.

EARLIER THAT AFTERNOON, BEFORE the radio show began, I had stopped by the Jean Lafitte National Historical Preserve/Acadian Cultural Center building right next door.

Jean Lafitte was a privateer and smuggler whose activities—illicit and otherwise—took him all through Cajun country. During the War of 1812 he offered his services to Gen. Andrew Jackson in the defense of New Orleans in exchange for a pardon for himself and his men. Jackson accepted, and Lafitte and his pirates fought with distinction. President James Madison pardoned the group, but after the war they returned to their old ways, preying upon shipping along the coast of Spanish America for several more years.

This afternoon, in the cultural center whose name honors him, there is to be a cooking demonstration. Cooking is perhaps the second cornerstone of Cajun culture, after music. In a kitchen set up with a stove and sink and an overhead mirror reflecting to the audience what's going on on the stovetop, Olga Manuel and Norma Jean Miller, local women, are demonstrating the preparation of crawfish étouffée. Louisiana produces something like 80,000 tons of crawfish each year.

Sugarcane planters in the 1700s began growing crawfish in small ponds and selling them in the French market in the late 1800s. They were thought of as a poor man's food until the 1960s, when they began to be fashionable. They have gills but can survive for six to seven months out of water, and live only about 18 months. Occasionally, especially during high-water periods, they migrate cross-country, making the highways slick and squishy. They are raised in ponds that are 8-to-18 inches deep and stocked at 25-to-50 pounds an acre. The ponds almost never have to be restocked.

"One pound of crawfish will serve three Cajuns or twenty Yankees," says Norma Jean, who describes herself as a crawfish farmer's wife. We get a taste of the finished étouffée, a spicy concoction of rice, onions, bell peppers, garlic, butter, and crawfish tails, and I make a date to come by Norma Jean's crawfish farm later in the week, even though, as she says, "We're mostly rice."

In the meantime, I explore some more of the region's back roads.

Pint-size prodigy Hunter Hayes, now eight, began playing a toy accordion at two and now performs at festivals, on national TV, and has just released his second CD. Here he performs and signs autographs for fans at the Boggy Bayou Festival in Pine Prairie.

Former rice farmers Lennis and Orphé Romero (opposite), 82 and 73, now perform Cajun songs for tourists beneath the Evangeline Oak in St. Martinville. Here Longfellow's fictional heroine disembarked from Nova Scotia, searching for her lover. The town, once called le Petit Paris, claims St. Martin de Tours Church (above), whose original sections date from 1765 and house gifts said to be from Louis XVI and Marie-Antoinette.

In his long poem *EVANGELINE*, which tells of the removal of the Acadians from their homes in Nova Scotia and their settlement in Louisiana, Longfellow writes of "…the maze of sluggish and devious waters," of the "towering and tenebrous boughs of the cypress" that "met in a dusky arch, and trailing mosses in mid-air.

"Lovely the moonlight was as it glanced and gleamed on the water," he wrote, and the sounds of wind and wave "mixed with the whoop of the crane and the roar of the grim alligator."

I don't find anything quite so dramatic, just fruit trees and azaleas in bloom, fields of sugarcane, and fishermen poised on the banks of the bayous. But in the charming little town of St. Martinville, once known as le Petit Paris and haven for aristocrats fleeing the French Revolution, Evangeline is still a presence. There's an Evangeline Funeral Home, but perhaps more appropriate is the Evangeline Oak, which, legends says, is the spot where the fictional Evangeline's boat docked when she arrived. Behind St. Martin de Tours Catholic Church, established in 1765, a statue of a pensive Evangeline sits, *(continued on page 64)*

Music and dance permeate Cajun life, especially on Sunday afternoons. Above, dancers dance at Angelle's Landing, and a fiddler fiddles (opposite) at a jam session in Eunice.

FOLLOWING PAGES: *Queenly contestants—including the Yam Queen, second from left, and Miss Ville Platte, center—gather at the Boggy Bayou Festival in the heart of Evangeline Parish. Cajun derives from a corruption of Acadian, a nod to the group's ancestors.*

gazing somberly off to her left, wearing wooden shoes and a cape and a severe hairdo. Dolores Del Rio played Evangeline in a 1929 silent film and later donated this bronze monument to St. Martinville.

In the shade beneath the Evangeline Oak I find the aged Romero brothers—Orphé, 73, and Lennis, 82—one playing an accordion, the other, a triangle. An upturned hat resting on a stool has some crumpled bills in it, so I add to it and request a song. "In French or English?" Lennis asks, in a thick Cajun drawl. I opt for French and am treated to "Jolie Blonde," "the number-one song in Louisiana." Toes tapping, they thump their way through it. I ask what the words mean. "It's about a pretty lady, a blonde," Orphé says. "She sings, 'You done left me to go far, far away. I have no more future, no more hopes. Dying is nothing, it's the suffering. That's what hurts. I'll love you until the day I die.'"

"That's a long time," says Lennis.

"You see, it's a very sad song," says Orphé.

I make my way, too, to a place called Jefferson Island, though it's not really an island. It sits 70 feet above sea level, perched atop a mammoth column of salt. Its Lake Peigneur was the scene of a bizarre incident in 1980. A Texaco rig, afloat on the lake and drilling into the lake bed below, inadvertently punctured the top of a huge salt dome—a dome hollowed out by decades of mining. Forty-eight miners were working in it at the time.

When the rig punctured the dome, water began draining out of the lake into the caverns and corridors below. The oil rig listed and sank. Fishermen in a motorboat found themselves suddenly aground with catfish leaping into the air around them. Barges carrying equipment and piles of rock salt disappeared down the churning vortex of a whirlpool. A tugboat, its engine running at full throttle, was dragged backward and disappeared into the whirlpool. The miners all managed to get out in time, though an estimated three-and-a-half billion gallons of water surged into their mine. Nine of the eleven lost barges eventually popped back to the surface as the lake refilled.

The place is quieter now, the lake refilled and placid. A wedding is being held on its banks, and the flautist is making the peacocks scream. I stroll through 20 acres of gardens, rich with live oaks and camellias and roses and daylilies.

I FIND MY WAY BACK TO NORMA Jean's farm near Eunice a few days later. She's a white-haired grandmother but full of boisterous, let's-go-take-a-look enthusiasm. We talk at her kitchen table. She calls her husband Bobby and their part-time helper Brother, though he is no relation to either of them. She has some expressions I find charming. She remembers hurricane Audrey. "It was 40 years ago. I remember because my son is 40 now and I was pregnant for him at the time." Oil rigs once were "going rickety-split." She calls okra "okry" and says that at certain times of the year "insects multiply like flies," then laughs when she realizes what she's said. She

*In Eunice, cook-off chefs compete in a Cajun specialty—étouffée. The mouthwatering
concoction of rice, onions, bell peppers, garlic, butter, and crawfish tails appears
in every home and on every restaurant menu.*

was educated as a medical technologist and hoped to become a doctor but chose
instead to get married, raise children, and farm rice, soybeans, and crawfish. I
ask her if it hurts when a crawfish catches you with his pincers. "Talk *about!*"

"Onions, bell peppers, and garlic—those are the holy trinity of Cajun
food," she says. "Really highly seasoned foods? That's not really Cajun cookin';
that's more Creole style. Lots of pepper, very hot. Cajun cookin' grew from
what people found down here, what they could find in their backyards. Onions,
bell peppers, stuff that would grow wild. But in New Orleans spices were
imported from the West Indies. That's Creole cookin'."

After the rice is harvested each year, ponds are flooded, and the crawfish
live and grow eating anything they can find, including the stubble, "so they
grow like crazy." Until around 1980 the rice and crawfish lands around Eunice
were planted with sweet potatoes and cotton and used for grazing cattle.

"A crawfish is a natural subsoiler. He burrows down so you end up with
a good fertilized area with no hardpan. Terrific. But you can't put out too many
or you end up with little bitty crawfish. People want big ones, so they don't
have to peel all day. If you peel eight hours and get 30 pounds of little ones
or 50 pounds of big ones, which do you want? Big ones, naturally. Everybody

and his brother has tried to develop a peeling machine, but so far it can't be done. They have to be peeled by hand."

Her big dog Snoopy dozes outside the screen door.

"China is the other big crawfish producing country. There's so much cheap labor there, they don't need a peeling machine. Seven pounds of live crawfish only gives you one pound of fish meat with 'fat' on, so it's not a cheap food."

I'm eager to see how you harvest crawfish, and Norma Jean says, "Let's go take a look!"

We pile into her car and go find Brother, who is about to empty and rebait several hundred traps that are spaced evenly a few yards apart in a flooded field. Their tops stick up a few inches above the surface of the water, like little chimneys. They are wire mesh and have two or three narrow funnel-shaped openings that crawfish can crawl into but have trouble finding their way out of. We're in a small flat-bottomed skiff that has a sort of paddle wheel at the back; the wheel rests on the bottom of the shallow pond and pushes us along. When we get under way, Brother reminds me of a one-armed paperhanger, for he is very busy. He steers using a foot pedal and controls the speed with his left hand, on a couple of levers, and, with his right hand, plucks traps from the water, empties the squirming crawfish into a bin, puts in a new piece of bait, and replaces the trap at the same time he lifts out the next one. The crawfish look like tiny lobsters. Brother is like a juggler. Norma Jean says, "To fish for crawfish you have to be ambidextrous. Your feet gotta work, your hands gotta work, and you can't worry about what's going on in between."

New regulations now forbid the vacuum-packing of crawfish by processors, which worries Norma Jean. "That will change the industry dramatically," she says. "Crawfish have a shelf life of only four or five days if they're not vacuum-packed."

Perhaps cajun country's most appealing back roads lie south and west of Lafayette in the marshlands and prairies along the coast.

On a warm, sunny day I head south on Rt. 35. The countryside is flat and rural, with small towns here and there. Rice fields stretch along both sides of the highway, and egrets stand in them, looking slim and elegant. South of Kaplan crawfish farms proliferate. Two men in a boat like Brother's are harvesting crawfish. There's a little town called Little Prairie. A bridge as high as a skyscraper crosses the Intracoastal Waterway, which is lined with big boats. Bayous reach in every direction; and cattle doze in barnyards, their legs tucked under them. Canals run along both sides of the highway and are lined with

Hoisting a wire-mesh trap, Ben Miller harvests crawfish on his grandfather's farm near Eunice. The creatures take three-to-five months to grow big enough to eat and seldom live longer than eighteen months. A rare white crawfish (below) emerges from one of Ben's traps.

FOLLOWING PAGES: *Signature of the balmy South, Spanish moss drapes a live oak. Evergreen and durable, its stately form lines avenues and graces gardens throughout the Gulf Coast region.*

willows, scrubby brush, and tall brown grasses aflutter with birds. You get the feeling that if you pulled a plug somewhere, this whole countryside would flood. Or drain.

In the town of Pecan Island, magnificent live oak trees are spaced along the front of a school. Beyond Pecan Island the landscape becomes even more boggy and marshy. Beautiful brown grasses reach eight or ten feet tall. A cormorant sits and spreads its ragged wings atop a pole, and a flock of 30 or so black-and-gray ducks bobs on a wind-ruffled bayou.

Westward along the bottom of Cameron Parish, fishing and hunting camps are on my right, marshland all the way to the ocean on my left. In Cameron I almost drive onto the wrong ferry, which would have taken me to Monkey Island. A friendly young woman turns me around and points me toward the ferry that crosses the narrow mouth of the Calcasieu River. I pay my dollar while gulls scream and a serious-sounding ship's horn sounds off to the left. Here comes *Lucky Lady,* a huge tanker out of Valletta, Malta. She passes right before us and looks like an apartment building going past. She's a-bristle with "No Smoking" signs, heading for the Port of Lake Charles.

At Holly Beach I turn north and soon find the Sabine National Wildlife Refuge. I stop for a look around, and a signboard tells me I may see buzzards, herons, terns, snowy egrets, white-faced ibis, alligators, moorhens, nutria, cottonmouths, snow geese, blue geese, widgens, blue-winged teals, northern shovelers, green-winged teals, and mallards. "Do Not Feed the Alligators," another sign warns, and I vow not to. The refuge, at 142,000 acres, is the largest waterfowl refuge on the Gulf Coast and was established in 1937 to preserve a large block of coastal marsh important to wintering geese and ducks. Waterfowl from both the Mississippi and Central Flyways winter on the refuge.

Beneath an overcast sky, I stroll along a path that winds across the marsh. Moorhens panic at my approach. Small alligators, with just their eyes and nostrils showing, swim by, their tails slowly swinging back and forth; they look like pull toys. A larger one, maybe six feet long, lies on a grassy bank. It watches me intently as I walk past. A flock of snow geese passes by overhead, and I walk through a flock of a hundred or so red-winged blackbirds. A warm breeze keeps the grasses nodding. But for the murmur of birds and insects, the silence is total.

The rest of the world seems very far away. ■

In a flurry of wispy feathers, an egret takes wing on Avery Island. Wading-bird populations are thriving and expanding in Louisiana, thanks to the development of the crawfish aquaculture industry over the last 50 years.

The Snowbelt

According to the weatherman, the windchill is 39° below zero. Fahrenheit. It's February in the snowbelt, and it feels it. The forests and lakes north of Duluth are frozen solid. It's a monochromatic world: naked black trees and bushes, glittery white snow. Thin white birches look cold. The occasional evergreen stands out like an exclamation point. Other flashes of color come from roadside signs: Mileage signs are green and white; adopt-a-highway signs, blue and white; signs for fishing resorts are every color.

I'm passing through gently rolling countryside and small towns. The road is hilly and curvy, just the way a back road should be. Roadsides are patterned with the busy tracks and trails of snowmobiles. They are as ubiquitous here as cattle in Texas or sunflowers in Kansas. People haul them around

behind their cars and pickups the way people in Kentucky tow horses.

A solitary crow goes flapping past. Little streams that the highway crosses are solid white sidewalks, some with animal, people, or snowmobile tracks. The highway is bumpy from the constant freezing and thawing. Trucks piled high with logs emerge from the forest, streaming trails of blown snow. There are no hitchhikers. Four snowmobiles come suddenly out of the woods, pause briefly while their drivers look both ways, then hurry across the highway. Others, on frozen lakes, are silenced by distance and look like lumpy hockey pucks sliding across the surface.

I'm HEADED FOR ELY, MINNESOTA, whose radio station terms itself "end-of-the-road radio," and indeed the area feels remote. One old-timer assures me that if you departed from Ely for the North Pole you'd cross only two highways on your way. Each summer some 200,000 canoeists come to Ely to paddle the nearby Boundary Waters Canoe Area Wilderness. But now it's wintertime, and in Whiteside Park in the center of town, the snow is flying. By the shovelful.

It's the time of Ely's winter festival, and the town is getting ready. More than 50 cubes of snow—perfectly shaped by plywood forms—have been deposited in the park by volunteers. Some are eight-feet-by-eight feet; others, four-by-four, and still others, eight-by-ten. They've been allowed to settle for several days and are now solid and ripe for carving. Bundled up in mittens, scarves, and parkas, snow sculptors are hard at work, armed with everything from picks and shovels to trowels and keyhole saws and currycombs. Shapes emerge: a kayaker, bears, a moose, an iguana, a remarkable skulking thief with haunted eyes and a bag over his shoulder. He is the work of Bob Maidl and will win the adult-single category at the judging. One of the largest cubes is being turned into an elaborate jail cell, complete with a reclining inmate—an old miner—reaching toward the naked woman he's dreaming about, while outside his dog stands on its hind legs, peering in a barred window. It's called Marcel's Big Night Out.

Teams of snow carvers come from all over the country—indeed, from all over the world. There are teams here from Canada and Argentina and another from Mexico. I chat for a moment with a girl from Buenos Aires. It's her fourth year. "The first year it was 60° below zero," she laughs. "I wondered, is it always going to be like this?"

Bearded voyageurs in authentic-looking costumes stand around a fire, over which bubbles a pot of split pea soup and ham hocks. The voyageurs josh with the tourists and deliver a steady patter: "Why do voyageurs eat such small breakfasts?" one asks. *(continued on page 82)*

Frozen canoeists run frozen rapids in an ice sculpture in Ely's Whiteside Park.
The Minnesota town's 1999 Voyageur Winter Festival drew scores of sculptors
from as far away as Buenos Aires and Mexico City.

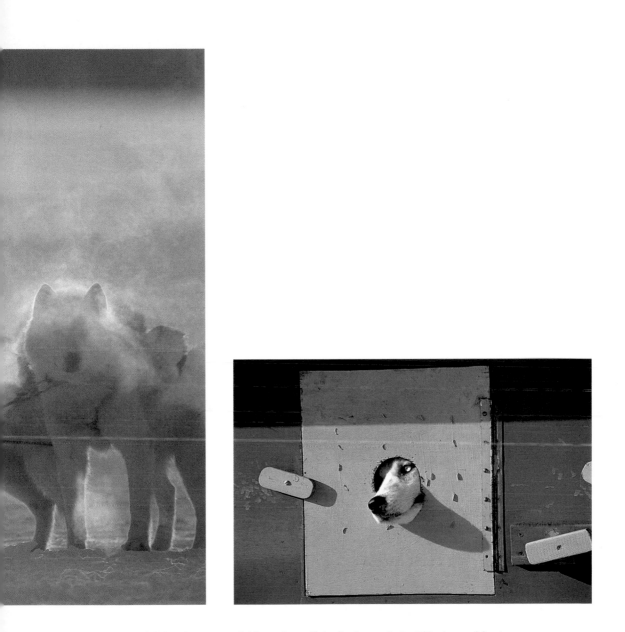

*Sled dogs, here to give children rides, puff clouds of vapor during Ely's winter celebration;
one, still penned, keeps an eye out for supper.*

FOLLOWING PAGES: *At Ely's Mukluk Ball, held in the community center,
some dancers stick to modern footwear; others sport the traditional mukluks—soft leather
boots with felt liners and rubberized soles.*

"Because one egg is *un oeuf*." The crowd groans.

Elsewhere around town, other events are taking place.

At the Trezona Trail, cross-country skiers are racing, towed by dogs. It's called skijoring, Norwegian for ski driving. A handful of shivering spectators watch, stamping their feet and burying their mittened hands deep in their parka pockets. There's a dark, overcast sky and a strong gusty wind. It's bitterly cold, but people are cheerful. The dogs are shaggy and tough, with pale blue-green eyes. Mike and his dog, Scout, win, covering the four miles in 19 minutes and 8 seconds. Their prize is 50 pounds of dog food. The dogs are barely puffing after having run four miles while pulling grown men.

Now small children strapped into snowshoes are racing; as they run, they kick up little puffs of snow from their shoes, like water from the tread of a tire. Several step on their own toes and sprawl forward onto their faces, then get up and gamely run some more. Adult snowshoe racers do a little better, though their course is more difficult, leading them across ditches and through underbrush. They collapse laughing in a heap at the finish line.

Then come the Mutt Races—sled dog races for little kids. "And don't call them dogsled races," says Emily Wahlberg, who is standing nearby and who has chaired the committee that puts on the winter festival for three years running. "It's not the sleds that race; it's the dogs." They race one at a time, against a clock. The sleds are shallow plastic tubs, each with a dog harnessed to it. Some of the dogs, new at this, don't know what's expected of them and peer at their shouting owners in confusion, wagging their tails hopefully.

That night there's a spaghetti dinner-dance in the community center. Several hundred people pass along a cafeteria line, then take their seats around long tables. Many are wearing down vests or sweaters.

Upstairs, from 8:00 p.m. until midnight, people dance to the Original Knights of Rock 'n' Roll, a fine band that plays all the standards from Elvis onward. The dance is billed as the Mukluk Ball, and people are supposed to wear mukluks, soft leather boots with felt liners and rubberized soles. Most of the mukluks have a fringe at calf-level that dances as furiously as the people. A few cheaters are wearing sneakers. There's a woman in a short black dress, but all the other women are wearing pants of one kind or another. After the ball, the cleanup crew finds a pair of long johns someone has left behind.

WHILE SNOW BLANKETS THE surface of northern Minnesota, a rarer commodity beneath the surface spurred the region's settlement in the first place. The tail end of the Vermilion Range touches Ely and its neighboring town, Soudan, where the Soudan iron-ore mine opened in 1882, the first in Minnesota. Its owner was a Harvard graduate from

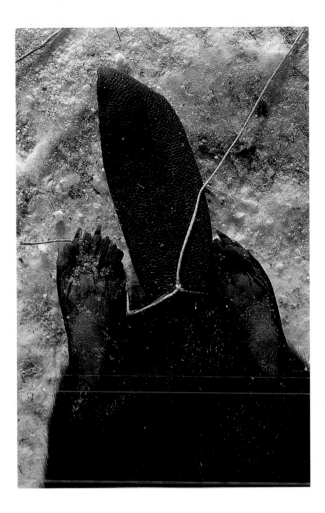

Now an ingredient, a beaver tail will soon be stew at the Voyageur encampment at Ely's winter festival. Costumed reenactors camp in the snowy park, cooking in the style of the region's early French-Canadian fur trappers.

Pottsville, Pennsylvania, named Charlemagne Tower. Within two years, ore was being shipped by train to Two Harbors, on Lake Superior, and by 1892 some 1,800 miners were employed in the mine. That year, 568,471 tons of iron ore were shipped to steel mills. The mine ceased production in 1962, and today only tourists visit. It's managed as the Soudan Underground Mine State Park.

Nancy Jamnick, whose great grandfather came to northern Minnesota from Austria, leads groups into the mine. She loads 30 or so of us—all topped by yellow plastic hard hats—into a double-decker elevator, and we drop through the darkness. Down down down, for three full minutes we descend, to the 27th level. Nancy's headlamp is our main source of light. The rattling elevator makes a terrific clatter, like a 1950s carnival ride. At the cool bottom—the temperature is a constant 52°F—tunnels run in either direction,

Jewels in a golden sea, the Apostle Islands lie sprinkled across some 720 square miles of Lake Superior, off Wisconsin's Bayfield Peninsula. Tracks on Lake Superior (opposite) mark the Ice Road, a winter route from Bayfield to Madeline Island, largest of the Apostles.

---

with railroad tracks down the middle. "There are 54 miles of tunnels down here," says Nancy. "We're about 2,341 feet below the surface—half a mile."

Swaying and bouncing, we ride for a mile or so in open-sided railroad cars, through tunnels dark but for occasional dim bulbs, a cool breeze in our faces. We disembark in a large stope, or dome. "This is hematite, very solid," says Nancy. "They didn't have to put up shoring; it's a very safe place to be."

She turns off the lights and we stand, trying to see our hands in front of our faces. There are several small children in our group, and Nancy calls them together and shows them how little candles fit into the miners' hats. "There were several different ethnic groups in town in those days," she tells them. "Most of the miners didn't speak English, or each other's language, either. They stayed within their ethnic groups at work. But the bosses split up the crews, mixing the different groups together. They thought if the men couldn't communicate, they wouldn't waste time talking. But you know what happened? The men learned each other's languages, and they became good friends."

"We're standing in a large dome," says Nancy. "But there's an even larger one 200 feet above our heads. I've been told it's 500 feet by 500 feet. But to get to it you have to crawl up 200 feet of wooden ladders. And

you know what happens to wood in 40 years? So I've never seen it."

High up in one corner of the dome a sort of noose is hanging from the ceiling. "What's the noose for," I ask Nancy. "That's for people who ask questions," she says. Actually, she goes on, it's for hanging pulleys to move heavy equipment.

She tells the children, "It's hard for us to imagine someone, like my great grandfather, leaving family and friends and moving halfway around the world. But within ten years of his arrival here, he had made enough money to buy a farm. The town was booming then. You didn't rent a room by the day, but by the shift. So when the day shift crawled out of bed, the night shift crawled in." Back into the elevators we go, for the ascent to the surface. Clanging and rattling, hurtling through the darkness, faster and faster, I feel like the charge in a roman candle, about to explode into the air.

O N A GRAY MORNING A FEW DAYS later, I head east from Ely into northern Wisconsin, passing first through Superior. It's an inland ocean port, connected by the St. Lawrence Seaway to the Atlantic Ocean. The day is balmy by northern standards, somewhere in the 30°s. A big snowfall in the night has dropped five or six inches of beautiful new

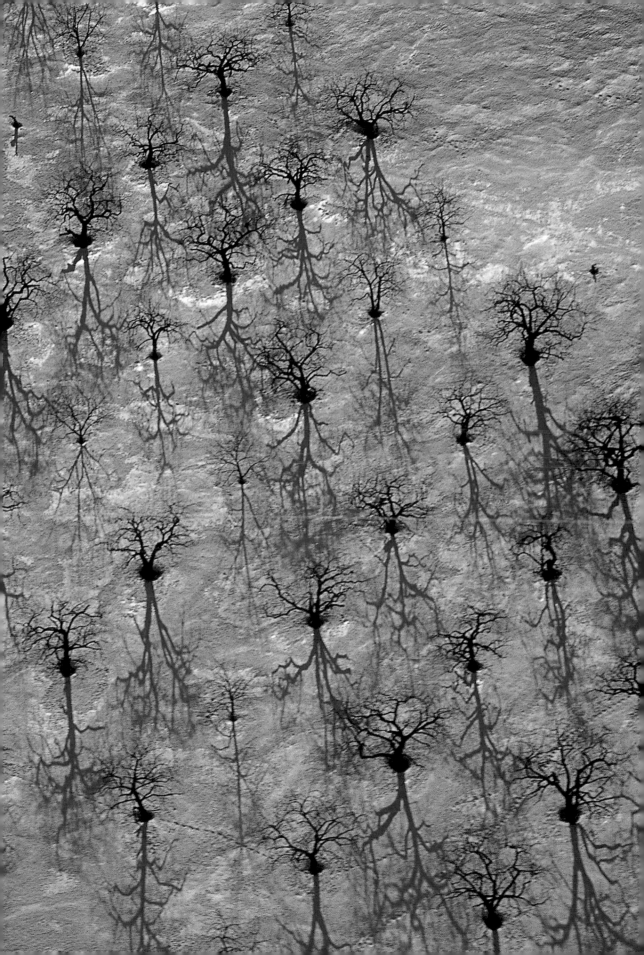

Snowmobile tracks (opposite) converge on a crossroads church in the Huron Mountains on Michigan's Upper Peninsula. In places here, snow is measured by the foot; it camouflages a truck (above) near Ontonagon at the base of the Keweenaw Peninsula.

white powder on the landscape; some clings to the branches of the pine trees. The highways have been plowed but not sanded, so the roadside snow is still pristine. Amateur plowers are doing their driveways with pickups and tractors. I meet a car with one green headlight and one yellow one; it reminds me of the sled dogs, some of whom have different-colored eyes. Towns I pass through are too small to have a Wal-Mart but big enough for a Main Street. The countryside is thick with state parks and national forests.

I head north toward the Apostle Islands, an archipelago of 22 islands that juts out into Lake Superior. In Ashland I visit the tidy JFK Memorial Airport, which honors the late President. It was the last place in Wisconsin he visited, shortly before his assassination, to see and talk about protecting the Apostle Islands.

Fur traders once plied the waters of the archipelago trapping beaver and building trading posts. Loggers denuded many of the islands in the late 19th and early 20th centuries, harvesting a mixed hardwood-conifer forest of hemlock, white pine, sugar maple, and yellow birch. The Midwest's growing cities were built of sandstone quarried from lakeside cliffs.

More than 150 species of birds flock to the Apostle Islands National Lakeshore; most—about 90 percent—migrate south for the winter. Loons send their demented yodels echoing across the islands.

Wisconsin Rt. 13 meanders north around the peninsula, passing in turn through Washburn and classy little Bayfield, and I set out to drive it. But the windblown snow is fierce and getting fiercer. The highway is snow-covered, with the parallel tracks of cars that have preceded me. Plumes of snow are blowing off the roofs of houses like the whiskers of spray that curl off breakers at the beach.

Bayfield—which prides itself on having escaped "fast food, amusement parks, traffic lights, and the fast lane," according to the Chamber of Commerce—is lost in a fog of swirling snow. I meet a snowplow making a giant plume of snow 40 feet above its cab. And a man clearing his driveway with a snowblower makes a towering cloud of snow that looks like Old Faithful. At Red Cliff the highway is slippery, and I'm creeping along at ten miles an hour. When all traces of the highway disappear in a whiteout I retreat.

Later, determined to come in from the cold, I find refuge in a barn-like hockey arena in Rice Lake, where a sectional high school hockey tournament is in progress. The Spooner Rails are meeting the New Richmond Tigers. Several thousand yelling, stomping fans are packed into the arena, filling every seat. I find a place to stand, up against the glass near one goal, shoulder to shoulder with hundreds of other standees. The woman beside me coughs continuously. "I've had a cold for seven weeks," she sniffs.

Hockey is a grand obsession here. The U.S. Hockey Hall of Fame in nearby Eveleth, Minnesota, is located at the juncture of U.S. 53 and Hat Trick Avenue. Much of its display honors the U.S. hockey team that defeated the Soviet Union for the gold medal at the 1980 Lake Placid Olympics. The puck that was in play at the end of the game is there, as well as the stick that Mike Eruzione used to score the winning goal.

Back in Rice Lake, the national anthem comes over the public address system, and everyone stands at attention, including the cheerleaders. They are in short skirts and regular shoes, so they walk across the ice very gingerly, flat-footed. They're wearing huge gloves, like oven mitts. According to my program, the Spooner cheerleaders are named April, Nikki, Kali, and Ingrid. I'm rooting for Spooner, only because it's the smaller town, population 2,464.

Banners of local merchants hang around the rink's perimeter: Southgate Quick Wash & Billiards, McDonalds, Pomps Tire Service, Dairy State Bank. A large U.S. flag and a smaller Canadian one hang from rafters over the ice.

When the game starts, I'm amazed at the quality of the skating. The skaters go very fast, frontward, backward, head over heels, sticks and puck flying. They collide with one another and with the Plexiglas wall, with a huge thump, four inches from my face. They go sprawling, sliding across the ice—arms, legs, and sticks all tangled together. The goalie's breath is

Sunday morning brunch brings a white-tailed deer to Eagle River on the Keweenaw Peninsula. In the harshness of winter, people here customarily help the deer, throwing out lettuce and other delicacies on Sunday mornings.

FOLLOWING PAGES: *Dusk falls on an outdoor hockey rink in St. Ignace, at the northern end of the Mackinac Bridge. Here, members of the Mites Division of the St. Ignace Outdoor Recreation League practice in late afternoon.*

visible as he crouches, waiting for the action to return to his end of the rink.

At the end of the first period, the Tigers lead 1-0. "Lots of parents don't want their kids to play hockey," says the man beside me, as we wait for play to resume, "because it's so expensive. A good pair of skates can be 300 dollars. I just paid 150 dollars for some for my 12-year-old, and they're *used.*"

There are no scores or penalties in the second period. "Hell of a game," says my neighbor. With two minutes left in the final period, and the Tigers leading 2-0, their fans begin chanting, "Start the bus! Start the bus!" They win, 3-1.

Huge chunks of county, state, and national forest lands sprawl across this part of Wisconsin, and they are a favored habitat of the omnipresent snowmobilers, who appear unexpectedly like buzzing gnats nearly everywhere you go. Hundreds of miles of groomed trails lace the forests—500 miles in Bayfield County alone—which

Rosy dawn tints snow-covered dunes along the Lake Superior shoreline. Magnificent dunes here have been growing for thousands of years, blown by off-lake winds and anchored by hardy, dune-building marram grass.

are blazed, marked, and maintained by the many snowmobile clubs that the aficionados join. They call them "snomo" trails, and they open each year in early December. These trails, many of which follow old forest service roads, qualify in my mind as byways, so I determine to try one.

One frosty but sunny morning, forest technician Bill Reardon bundles me into rented boots, suit, gloves, and helmet for a day trip into the Nicolet National Forest. I've never ridden a snowmobile, so am looking forward to it.

We truck the machines to the campground at Anvil Lake, east of the town of Eagle River, and set off on a rough and winding trail. Eagle River is home to the Snowmobile Racing Hall of Fame and Museum and displays "ancient" snowmobiles from 1967.

Our snowmobiles are noisy and bumpy and leave behind them a faint odor of internal combustion engine. We twist and turn, up hill and down, through the forest, sometimes on the bed of an old railroad track, sometimes on a new rails-to-trails pathway, but mostly on old forest service roads.

The new head of the U.S. Forest Service, former fishing guide Michael Dombeck, was born in the lake country of northern Wisconsin and grew up in the Chequamegon National Forest. He recently has gotten the attention both of environmentalists and forest industry officials with his move to reduce the number of roads in the national forests. There are some 383,000 miles of timber roads in the national forests now. Most of them offer access for recreationists, but many are degrading watersheds, filling streams with silt, and destroying wildlife habitats.

Bill and I stop now and then to talk and to let the noise of the machines die out. At one stop, Bill spots the tracks of a fisher in the snow. "They're kind of a problem," he says. "They kill people's house cats. Wolves have come back to northern Wisconsin naturally, from Minnesota. The wildlife people were hoping we'd get 80 or so wolves in the state, but now we have a couple of hundred."

For a while we're on the track of the Thunder Lake Narrow Gauge Railroad, built at the turn of the century for logging. "These are mostly hardwood forests," Bill tells me, "and since hardwood logs don't float, they had to build a railroad to get the logs out of the forest."

Green daubs of paint on some of the trees—applied by Bill—indicate which trees will be cut, mostly spruce. Blue paint marks the border between units of the forest. "This plantation was planted by the CCC around 1935. It became a national forest in 1933."

When we shut down the machines, the stillness is total except for the cawing of a crow. There are otter tracks alongside the trail. It appears the animal was dragging its tail. "No," says Bill, "he was sliding on his stomach. They'll run through the woods and when they come to a slope, they'll flop down on their bellies and slide."

Driving the snowmobiles requires concentration, but when I get a chance to look into the forest, the scene is lovely: dark trees and shadows, the snow white and undisturbed.

THE SNOW THAT THE SNOWMOBILers so prize falls frequently here in the winter. A few days later, it begins in mid-afternoon, softly at first, then with more determination, until clouds of snow swirl in the wind. Pellets of snow patter like sand against the back of my parka hood as I hurry to a motel office. The snow piles higher and higher— two inches, four inches, six inches. Traffic lights grow dim through the falling snow. It snows through the night, and in the morning there is a world transformed. Drifts two feet deep surround my car, but the snowmobilers, out early, are in heaven.

Officials once salted the highways to speed the melting of the snow, but the salt attracted deer, which were killed by the thousands by traffic. So highway officials now mix sand with the salt. It blackens the snow but the deer don't like the taste, so they tend to stay away from the highway edges.

*First-time fisherman Scott Burns, Jr., doffs mittens but keeps his hat on as
he checks his line at the Big Bay Fishing Derby. Scott's great great grandfather established
the original settlement at Big Bay, then called Burns Landing.
Sadly, Scott caught nothing this day. Opposite, winter frosts the edges of Pictured Rocks
National Lakeshore, eroded cliffs on the south shore of Lake Superior.*

The Upper Peninsula of Michigan—or the U.P., where the Yoopers live—
is rimmed by lakes: Lakes Superior, Michigan, and Huron draw a continuous,
1,700-mile shoreline around the U.P. Most of the peninsula reaches farther
north than Montreal. Snow is piled so high along the highways that I can see
the motel signs but not the motels. Some years, I'm told, residents impale
orange tennis balls on the tips of their car radio antennae so other drivers will
see them coming out of driveways and around corners.

Near Marquette, a small group of snowmobilers is assembling alongside
the highway in bright, gaudy uniforms that make them look like a flock of
exotic birds. Marquette, home to a lively university, has also been the main
shipping port for the region's iron ore since the middle of the 19th century.
Its Maritime Museum displays—among other artifacts—the birch-bark canoe
used by Charles T. Harvey while building the first lock at Sault Ste. Marie.
The university claims the world's largest wooden dome, the Superior Dome.
It's as high as a 14-story building and encloses 5.1 acres under its fir roof.

I drive north on the Keweenaw Peninsula on U.S. Rt. 41 toward Houghton
as the day warms and a thick blanket of fog descends. *(continued on page 102)*

Two facts of life in the snowbelt: snow and snowmobiles. A blizzard off Lake Superior
barely fazes snowmobilers in the Porcupine Mountains (above, left), and predawn
finds another group preparing for an 80-mile run from Silver City to Houghton (above).

FOLLOWING PAGES: *Cheerful lights beckon the hardy to a resort in tiny Paradise,*
Michigan—a name some winter visitors might take issue with.

There's a snow thermometer on the peninsula, a tall, wooden, red-white-and-black edifice that sticks up out of the snow. There's a mark every foot to track the snow depth each year. The record was set in the winter of 1978-79, when the thermometer logged more than 32 feet—*feet!*—of snow.

Lake Superior, on my right, is speckled with dozens of ice fishermen and their huts. There's no snow on the lake, just ice, so all the men are moving very gingerly. Farther along, there's a cluster of huts on the ice that looks like a village. The ice fishermen are a puzzle to me. Can the pleasures really outweigh the discomforts?

Doug Plivelich, a student at Northern Michigan University in Marquette, and two of his friends, Andy Weaver and Quinlan Henry, loan me a pole and take me fishing on a blustery, gray morning. We trudge out onto Teal Lake. Doug is a big, blond rugby player studying construction technology.

He says, "If you fall through the ice, stick your arms out like a scarecrow. That'll save you." I say, "If I fall through the ice, the terror alone will kill me."

The boys have an auger, powered by a three-horsepower engine that starts like a lawn mower. It makes a hole 11 inches across through 3 feet of ice in just a couple of minutes. Slush and pale blue water come boiling up out of the hole. We drill half a dozen holes and over several place a tip-up—a little erector-set gizmo that waves a tiny orange flag when a fish bites. Doug has one 50 years old that belonged to his grandfather. A bait bucket is full of tiny silver suckers. Everyone takes a plastic bucket, overturns it next to a hole, drops a line and hook in, turns his back to the wind, and sits and fishes.

I may as well admit it here: No fish were harmed during the writing of this chapter.

The wind, blowing across acres of ice, is bitterly cold, and after a few hours we give up. "Unlucky," says Doug. "Usually you catch *something.*"

THE NEXT DAY I HEAD EASTWARD along the top edge of the U.P. into a gray and cloudy morning. Little bursts of sleet patter at my windshield, and a big flock of crows, feeding on a deer carcass at roadside, lift off as I pass.

It's just a few miles from here, on Whitefish Point, that the Great Lakes Shipwreck Historical Museum, now closed for the winter, tells the story of the many mishaps that have befallen ships on Lake Superior, one of the most dangerous bodies of water on Earth. And it's only about 17 miles off Whitefish Point that one of the most famous sinkings occurred: During one of the worst Great Lakes northers of the century the *Edmund Fitzgerald,* of legend and song, sank in just a few minutes in the early evening of November 10, 1975, taking all of her 29 crewmen with her. "Does anyone know

Winter seems a benign and beautiful presence from inside a bakery in Paradise.
On the table awaits a pasty, a popular local staple. The small pie, made from a meat
and vegetable mixture, is baked like a turnover.

where the love of God goes when the waves turn the minutes to hours?" sang Gordon Lightfoot, in his song, "The Wreck of the Edmund Fitzgerald."

Eastward I go, through a pastoral landscape. Magnificent sand dunes line the shores of the U.P., where the ingredients for dunes exist: sand, vegetation, currents, and wind. Together they have built the largest collection of freshwater coastal dunes in the world, part of the scenery here for 3,000 or 4,000 years.

Little towns come and go: Forest Lake and Wetmore, Shingleton and Seney and Trout Lake. Finally I come to the lovely swoop of Mackinac Bridge. It's five miles long, and its towers rise 552 feet above the straits, where whitecaps on the slate-gray water nudge big sheets of ice that reach out from the shores. The wind is howling across the bridge, and trucks creep along at 20 miles an hour with their blinkers blinking. On especially windy days, the bridge bows sideways as much as 20 feet.

In a peppery little snowstorm I cross over the bridge and, like one of those migrating birds, head south.

Next stop: the much warmer forested hills and hollows of the Cumberland Plateau. ∎

Heart of the Cumberland

GIVING DIRECTIONS on the phone, Fred Lewis says, "Head for the end of the world, and when you get there, you're here." Following those directions, I follow ever smaller highways deeper into the hills of eastern Kentucky. I make a hard, almost U-turn, steeply downward onto Fred's drive, park the car, honk the horn—again, as per instructions—and walk across a narrow bridge. Fred, with a magnificent fluffy white beard, is sitting in the shade looking down on the gurgling Big Laurel Creek. From a kennel somewhere out back, dogs are barking. Ducks in the creek appear to be dozing.

Fred is the owner, operator, and sole employee of the Lewis Mountain Museum, near Big Laurel. He is 78 now, and recovering from a recent cataract operation, so is slowing down some.

Over the years, he has built several wooden cabins to house his collection of Appalachian artifacts and memorabilia. He shows me an old grindstone that he refers to as if it were feminine, like a ship: "She's about 200 years old," he says of the stone. "See? She's got these little grooves to channel the ground grain off the edge."

You can't tour Fred's collection without being reminded that this is coal country. He has two small, fragile, wooden bird cages, the sort miners used to carry a canary with them into the mines to detect bad air. "If the air was bad, the canary would die," says Fred. He also has a terrific collection of old scrip, the currency used by coal mines to pay their miners. "There were 250 mines in Harlan County alone," Fred tells me, "all using different scrip. So you were forced to buy your groceries from your particular mine's company store."

KING COAL. THE SUBSTANCE HAS been a blessing and a curse to the Appalachians. Nearby Harlan developed as a shipping point for lumber and coal when the railroad arrived in 1911 and between 1900 and 1938 was the scene of violent labor disputes involving miners and the operators of the local coal mines. Their brawls earned the town the name of Bloody Harlan and played a large role in the development of organized labor.

Driving today through the peaceful countryside, it's easy to forget that the plateau is underlain by huge deposits of high-quality coal, low in ash and sulfur, high in heat content. It is by far Kentucky's most important mineral, though development of new fuels during the 20th century has lessened the demand for it. Where once it accounted for about 90 percent of North America's energy, today it counts for less than 25 percent.

The mining of coal has not been a benign activity on the plateau. Demand for millions of wooden props to shore up the mines helped to destroy the forests. And the largest customer of Kentucky coal—the Tennessee Valley Authority, or TVA—has contributed to the problems: Bound by law to get the cheapest coal possible, its policies promoted the rise of strip-mining, the most economical way of mining. As subterranean mines couldn't compete with the strip-mines, miners lost their jobs and moved to cities. As technological advances came, fewer men could mine more coal, so even more miners lost their jobs.

The people of the region were helpless to stop the strip-mining. Their ancestors had signed away the mineral rights to their lands, often for a few cents an acre. The contracts bound the sellers and their "heirs, successors and assigns forever," which is a long time. Further, the deeds allowed the mineral owner to extract coal by any method "deemed necessary or convenient." And beginning around 1950, strip-mining certainly came to be the most "convenient."

In the mid-1960s the President's Appalachian *(continued on page 114)*

Cumberland Falls drops a silver curtain across its namesake river in Kentucky. The Cumberland was the Shawnee until renamed in 1750 by Thomas Walker for the Duke of Cumberland, allegedly because the crookedness of the channel reminded him of the Duke.

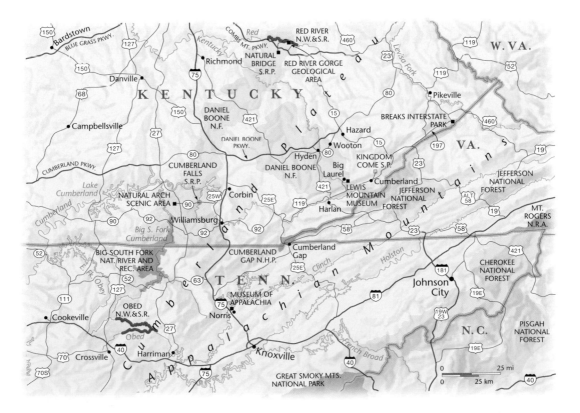

With a little help from a friend, a climber (opposite) inches up a cliff face in Red River Gorge Geological Area in Kentucky. More than 100 natural stone arches have formed in the area's 27,000 acres, including Skybridge (above).

FOLLOWING PAGES: *Waters of Eagle Falls drop into a cool and mossy gorge on their way to join the Cumberland.*

Regional Commission declared, "Much of the wealth produced by coal and timber was seldom seen locally. It went downstream with the great hardwood logs; it rode out on rails with the coal cars; it was mailed between distant cities as royalty checks from non-resident operators to holding companies.… Even the wages of local miners returned to faraway stockholders via company houses and company stores."

The commission turned to building roads to stimulate the failing economy of the region; some 2,000 miles of new pavement crisscrossed the region.

In his classic *Night Comes to the Cumberland,* Harry M. Caudill chronicled the devastation strip-mining visited upon his home state. "Coal has always cursed the land in which it lies," he wrote. "When men begin to wrest it from the earth it leaves a legacy of foul streams, hideous slag heaps and polluted air. It peoples this transformed land with blind and crippled men and with widows and orphans. It is an extractive industry which takes all away and restores nothing. It mars but never beautifies. It corrupts but never purifies."

Sitting now with Fred Lewis, watching the ducks drift slowly by on Big Laurel Creek, I admire the clarity of the water. Fred says, "It's clear today but some days it's muddy—when they're strippin' upstream. You can always tell."

Pulling out of fred's hidden drive, I reflect on his region, the heart of the Cumberland Plateau. Life is more hidden here, I think; I have the feeling that the back roads are passing by fascinating people and places, but the forest and the hollows and the mountains keep them private. The land has been horribly scarred over the decades by logging, farming, and strip-mining, but much of the destruction is invisible from the roads. A green curtain hides much that goes on here.

The Cumberland Plateau is a rumpled but basically flat tableland that stretches northeast-to-southwest from southern West Virginia to northeastern Alabama. It averages some 2,000 feet above sea level and some 50 miles in width. Structurally, it's the western section of the Appalachian Mountains. Its heart lies in eastern Kentucky and northeastern Tennessee, near where the two states touch southwestern Virginia. The Cumberland Gap, in Tennessee, is the heart's aorta.

An early surveyor named Thomas Walker, hired to stake a grant beyond the Blue Ridge, named the Cumberland River for the Duke of Cumberland, George II's son. The name eventually attached itself to the river, the plateau, the gap, several counties, cities and towns, a sound, a road, a peninsula, a lake, an island, and a large cave system in Warren County in central Tennessee.

Early immigrants included Scotch-Irish and Germans, as well as Revolutionary War veterans who were granted millions of acres of Cumberland

Warm and inviting, a rural church in Tennessee offers an open door and a spiritual fellowship. In pioneer days, Presbyterian ministers helped settlers face the hazards of nature and Indians, but Baptists now easily outnumber them.

lands by the Military Reservation Act of 1782. They encountered Cherokee and Shawnee Indians, who up until then had had the plateau to themselves.

In places the tableland is fairly flat; in others, mountains rumple its surface. It is remote and sparsely populated, covered with second-growth forests, graced with waterfalls, gouged by canyons. Hundreds of thousands of acres have been set aside in parks, recreation areas, state natural areas, state and national forests, and national monuments and landmarks.

Natural Bridge State Resort Park features a sandstone arch that spans 80 feet and clears 65 feet, one of the largest on the plateau. The park is adjacent to the Red River Gorge Geological Area, part of the Daniel Boone National Forest. The Red River was approved for damming by the Corps of Engineers in 1962, but protests stopped it before it could be built. Today the 27,000-acre area features towering cliffs, rock shelters, and more than 100 natural arches.

The Breaks Interstate Park straddles the Kentucky-Virginia border and holds what local people claim is the deepest canyon east of the Mississippi River. In 1915 the Clinchfield Railroad completed a line through the breaks that had 20 tunnels in 35 miles of track.

Kingdom Come State Park honors the fictional *(continued on page 120)*

Honey Creek (above) tumbles toward the Big South Fork River. The Honey Creek "pocket wilderness," established by a southern paper company, is now under federal management. Morning fog fills the valleys below Kingdom Come State Park (above, right). Kentucky author John Fox, Jr., used this region as the setting for The Little Shepherd of Kingdom Come.

FOLLOWING PAGES: *Bluegrass jam session fills the living room of Sherman Wooton's home. Son Paul, at left, plays the guitar while grandson Ishi, nine, fiddles and Brian Godchaux plays the mandolin.*

High spirits prevail at the 9th Annual Red Mule Bluegrass Festival in Relief, Kentucky. These energetic cloggers have the right moves if not the right footwear for the traditional Appalachian dance, named for wooden-soled shoes.

hero of *The Little Shepherd of Kingdom Come*, a Civil War novel by Kentuckian John Fox, Jr. Pine Mountain State Resort Park features a famous chained rock— a huge boulder facetiously held in place by a large chain that keeps it from toppling onto the town of Pineville. It has been a tourist attraction since 1933, when the Pine Mountain Chained Rock Club, the Boy Scouts, and members of the CCC wrapped the chain around it and anchored it to the mountain.

In Tennessee, four rivers protected as part of the Obed Wild and Scenic River thread a forested canyon in the central plateau with walls 200 to 400 feet high in places. Straddling the Kentucky-Tennessee border southwest of Cumberland Falls is the Big South Fork National River and Recreation Area, which features some of the best white-water rafting and canoeing in the Southeast.

Cumberland Falls itself is on the move. Geologists say it has inched upstream probably 40 miles over millions of years. It is about 68 feet high and 125 feet wide in summer, with a flow of 30,000 cubic feet per second in flood. It produces a famous phenomenon if conditions are right—a "moonbow," the nocturnal counterpart of a rainbow. On cloudless nights with a full moon shining and enough water flowing over the falls to produce a mist, a white light sometimes forms at the base of the falls, looms up, and arcs downstream with the breeze. I visit the falls on a sunny day and am rewarded with a rainbow. It's a summer afternoon, and several hundred people are visiting the park with children and dogs in tow. We stand at the overlook, safely behind railings, and take turns photographing one another with the falls at our backs. The rainbow dances and sways with the breeze. Stone steps lead downward to the cool and shady base. Among the first white men to see the falls was a party of boatmen led by Zachariah Green in 1780. When they arrived, they found their boat too large to portage, so they sent it over the falls by itself. It survived, to their great pleasure, bobbing unbroken in the pool below the falls.

T HESE EARLY PIONEERS IN THE Cumberland, like those up and down the entire Appalachian chain, were a hardy and resourceful lot who began a tradition alive today: craftsmanship. To them, craft was necessity. With no manufactured goods to speak of, they made their own. Furniture was produced in the home, by the homeowner. Pottery and crockery emerged from local clay, shaped by local hands. Worn clothing became quilts.

Fifty or sixty miles to the east of Cumberland Falls, in another section of Daniel Boone National Forest, I find a lean and bearded craftsman, 89-year-old Sherman Wooton, who lives just outside Hyden, Kentucky. He has been making rough and rugged walnut chairs since 1974. His small home and workshop cling to the bank of Citation Creek and are reached from a gravel drive, via a homemade, one-person-at-a-time wooden bridge across the creek.

His workshop illustrates a rule I've encountered before: The untidier a craftsman's workshop, the more beautiful the objects that emerge from it. Sherman's is a mess, piled with pieces of lumber in various stages of preparation, chairs partly built or completed but for a coat of varnish, bits and pieces of leftover projects. "I don't have a ruler or anything," he tells me. "I don't measure. I just go to work. The design comes out of my head. There's no nails. Just glue and pegs. The joint tightens as it shrinks and dries."

I ask how he learned to make chairs. "When I was a kid, we lived way down on Hell for Certain Creek, and when it was time for me to go to school, my dad sent me to board at the Pine Mountain Settlement School. I was there until I was 18. They had an Italian man who was a carpenter and a stonemason, and he trained us boys—how to make furniture and put in windows and things they're not teaching in schools any more."

An American flag hangs by Sherman's door, and a bird feeder dangles from the bridge. It takes him several weeks to make a chair, and he sells them as fast as he can build them. For between $600 and $1,000 each. "I sent one of my chairs to Nixon when he was President, but never heard from him," he says.

Gleaming simplicity distinguishes the work of Matthew Boggs, teacher of woodworking at the Pine Mountain Settlement School in Harlan County, Kentucky. Appalachian crafts, famous around the world, began with pioneers making what they needed.

Are your chairs similar to those the pioneers built for themselves a hundred years ago? I ask him. "Well, I'd say pretty much so. I use the same techniques and the same tools they used." He uses a shaving knife to strip his lumber and a carpenter's bench to hold it steady. "Workin' at the bench keeps my arms in pretty good shape," he says.

I'm sitting in one of his chairs, in the shade, with Citation Creek murmuring at my elbow. It's cool and pleasant and I'm reluctant to leave. I ask him how many chairs he has built since 1974. "I have no idea," he says, and sitting here in the peace and quiet I can see why such record keeping might seem irrelevant.

THE APPALACHIANS, THOUGH NOT tall and rugged like western mountains, still presented a barrier to westward settlement. One way through was via the Cumberland Gap. No one really "discovered" the gap. Native Americans followed bison and deer through it, and called it the Warrior's Path, for it connected the Shawnee and Cherokee Nations. European settlers followed the Indians. Daniel Boone spent several years exploring the country around the gap, and in 1775 led a party of 30 men who blazed the Wilderness Trail from the gap into Kentucky. Immigrants

Eva Tussey of David, Kentucky, quilted for—"Oh Lordy! years and years!"—before failing health forced a halt. A local craft center sold several of her quilts, but "they wanted 35 percent of the take, so I gave most of 'em to my children."

followed, and by the end of the Revolutionary War about 12,000 people had crossed into the western territory. By 1792, when Kentucky became a state, its population exceeded 100,000.

I head for the gap on Rt. 92, going east. Early morning fog is lifting, leaving the haze that gives the blue to the Blue Ridge Mountains. The highway is winding and narrow, passing sometimes beneath a green canopy, sometimes alongside peaceful farms. Still, dark streams reflect the trees and sky overhead, and rocky bluffs look naked where the highway has been blasted through them. Rt. 92 is like a gentle roller coaster, up and down, around and around.

From Pinnacle Overlook, in the Cumberland Gap National Historical Park, off Rt. 25E, you can see, far below, how the gap acted as a sort of funnel for pioneers. Three states—Kentucky, Virginia, and Tennessee—touch noses here. A tunnel carries a steady stream of traffic between Kentucky and Tennessee.

In 1893 historian Frederick Jackson Turner recognized the importance of the gap. "Stand at Cumberland Gap," he wrote, "and watch the procession of civilization, marching single file—the buffalo following the trail to the salt springs, the Indian, the fur-trader and hunter, the cattleraiser, the pioneer farmer—and the frontier has passed by."

Watermelons tempt buyers (above) to a Crossville, Tennessee, parking lot. Bluegrass musician Carlock Stooksbury (opposite) plays the mouth organ at the Museum of Appalachia.

FOLLOWING PAGES: *In vibrant greens, summer comes to Grassy Cove, Tennessee, near the southern end of the Cumberland Plateau, a region of more traditional farmland.*

The Cumberland Plateau reaches far down into Tennessee, and I follow where it leads—through river valleys and thick forests, through small towns that shoulder aside the Interstates to make do on their own. The people are warm and courteous, the cattle placid in their bovine indifference.

THE APTLY NAMED MUSEUM OF Appalachia lures me to Norris, Tennessee. When I arrive for my visit, a mother hen and her six fluffy chicks come strolling up to my car door, on the off chance that I might have some bugs with me. A depraved looking black-and-white goat leers at me from its spot on the wrong side of its fence. I tour the museum, trying to take in as much as I can. Kindergarten children in matching white T-shirts, holding hands two by two, proceed me. Displays fill cases and cover walls and hang from ceilings. I get the feeling that here is everything that ever had anything to do with any part of any kind of life in this part of the Cumberland Plateau.

I rest my aching feet for a while on the porch of one of the cabins. On a similar porch on the next cabin over, a small band—a fiddle, a guitar, a banjo,

a hammer dulcimer—are playing old country songs. "Nothin' like pickin' on a porch," one of the musicians says. I recognize "The Battle of New Orleans" and "Seeing Nellie Home." A cool breeze floats off the meadow, and I sit and let it wash over me along with the music. A peacock screams.

Over a lunch of meat loaf and mashed potatoes and gravy, the museum's founder-director John Rice Irwin tells me, "As a child I was more interested in the older people, my grandparents, for instance, and the elderly of the community. They knew I was interested in things that belonged to their grandparents, so they started giving me a few little items." So began John Rice's collection, which has now grown into hundreds of thousands of items displayed in 30 or so buildings on 65 acres of rural Anderson County northwest of Knoxville.

I ask him about the inscription I had seen in the museum: "What better way is there to know a people than to study the everyday things they made, used, mended and cherished, and cared for with loving hands." He tells me, "I have tried to furnish the buildings and rooms as if the family has just strolled down to the spring to fetch the daily water supply."

He collected most of the artifacts shown himself, traveling up and down the region's hills and hollows. "Absolutely," he says. "I used to go door to door, house to house. Sometimes now I go back into the mountains to some hollow and I'll begin to realize, hey, I've been here before.

Information contained in the hundreds of hand-lettered captions next to most of the artifacts was compiled by John Rice himself. "It's the stories that make these artifacts come to life," he says. "For instance, I was at a public auction once. There was an old homemade bucket offered and nobody bid, nobody wanted it. But in passing, someone mentioned that it had been fished out of the river during the Barren Creek Flood, one of the most devastating floods we ever had. It occurred to me that, if you knew the history of the bucket, it would be of some importance; if you didn't know the history, it would be just another old bucket. So I bought it."

I tell John Rice that among the things I admire most in his museum is a mousetrap that is the soul of ingenuity. When a mouse enters the cage, the door slams shut behind it. But as the mouse makes its way farther into the trap, it slides down a skid and falls into another section of the trap, which reopens the door behind it so another mouse can get in. "People in these mountains have long had this Snuffy Smith, hillbilly image that is simply not correct. People here were full of ingenuity and intelligence," he says.

Farther down in tennessee, I devote a day to antiquing and browsing in the Cumberland General Store south of Crossville. It's a wonderland of old-time miscellaneous merchandise.

*With little to fear from traffic, a Grassy Cove mutt takes the middle of
the road. Such quiet country byways vein the heart of the Cumberland, leading
always to the unexpected, the traditional, or the sublimely scenic.*

Shelves groan with everything from cast-iron sugar kettles to goose quill pens,
from yo-yos to adzes, from bottle cappers to farrier tools.

In Crossville itself I find the Plateau Livestock Exchange, where on Saturdays farm animals are auctioned. Local farmers sit in a semicircular gallery
surrounding a pit into which cattle are driven one at a time. The auctioneer's
patter I find hypnotic and I sit for a while. The farmers, about 30 of them,
are poker-faced as they bid, sometimes with the merest movement of a hand.
I sit very still, lest I inadvertently buy something. Backstage, the scene is hot,
smelly, confused, and very noisy.

Across the highway is Crossville's other major attraction: the Crossville
Flea Market, billed as Tennessee's largest. Several rows of booths, most nicely
shaded by tall trees, offer everything that flea markets usually offer—and then
some. Thousands of people stroll among them, looking for bargains. "I could
probably use a bunch of this stuff, if I knew what I needed," says a man to
his wife.

I don't find anything to buy, but I stroll the afternoon away among the
citizens of Crossville. "A southerner talks music," Mark Twain wrote, and
I listen to their singing. ∎

Sand Hills and Prairies

I T'S THE FOURTH OF July, and I'm late. I had hoped to be in North Platte in time for the fireworks, but here it is dusk and we're just leaving Denver. Our tiny, low-flying commuter plane, with just 12 or so passengers, wings eastward into the gathering darkness, and, as I peer from my window, I see a wondrous thing: From the small scattered towns on the prairie, sudden mushrooms of red and green lights burst in the darkness.

Fireworks!

We travelers are transfixed, glued to our windows. And as we descend into North Platte, the pilot banks and turns, and the town passes by my window. From a dozen places, all over the city, fireworks are climbing into the sky, blossoming flowers and trailing streaks, bursts of soundless color.

I think: Welcome to Nebraska!

The northwestern corner of the Cornhusker State, treated as a mere pathway to the West by many in our history, is for me a destination. Its broad vistas and big skies, its small towns and mammoth ranches, its courteous, shy people, its back roads and byways all appeal to me. Here are the sand hills, 19,000 square miles of grass-stabilized dunes, one of the largest such regions in the world. They were formed by blowing sand more than 5,000 years ago; some are 400 feet high and up to 20 miles long. This is no desert; a huge groundwater reservoir underneath the dunes rises to the surface in many places, creating marshes, ponds, and wetlands. Many early immigrants passed the sand hills by, but later pioneers found them perfect for raising cattle.

Some fine writers have come from here—Wright Morris, Mari Sandoz, and Willa Cather among them. On the brutally difficult time of the early pioneers, Cather wrote, of one of her young heroes: "…the great fact was the land itself, which seemed to overwhelm the little beginnings of human society that struggled in its sombre wastes…he felt that men were too weak to make any mark here, that the land wanted to be let alone, to preserve its own fierce strength, its peculiar, savage kind of beauty, its uninterrupted mournfulness."

I BEGIN MY VISIT AT BROKEN BOW, north and west of Kearney. On Rt. 30, as you leave one small town you can see the grain elevator of the next one rising in the distance. A railroad track, busy with coal trains, runs alongside the highway. The trains sound their horns on falling notes at each of the frequent crossings. Those going west toward Wyoming are empty; the ones heading east are piled high with coal. It's a hot July day. Cattle in the fields huddle in the shade of whatever tree is available to them, and puffy white clouds pile up overhead.

Lunchtime finds me devouring the day's special at a café in Callaway— a hot roast beef sandwich with salad bar and a cup of soft ice cream, $4.95. Every farmer and workman in the county seems to be here, and the two waitresses are frantic.

Broken Bow, population 3,778, is the seat of Custer County, which was the heart of sod-house country. Called "prairie marble," sod was used here to build schools and homes and some businesses, as well as corrals, henhouses, corncribs, windbreaks, and pig pens. One pioneer even built a two-story sod house. American barns, in pioneer days, much resembled their European forebears, and log houses derived from Scandinavia, but the sod house is indigenous to the American plains and is found nowhere else. Cather wrote of these early homes, "you did not see them until you came directly upon them. Most of them were built of the sod itself, and were only the unescapable ground in another form." (continued on page 140)

Ignited by the setting sun, the sky above the Niobrara National Wildlife Refuge blazes. Fort Niobrara, built here in 1879, kept the peace between settlers and nearby Sioux.

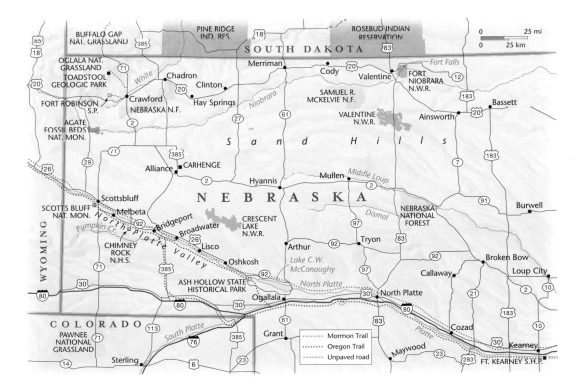

Nothing funny about riding an infuriated bull, in spite of the presence of a clown (above, right). A common weekend event in western Nebraska, rodeos grew from an authentic cowboy tradition. This one, part of the 33rd Annual Callaway Pioneer Picnic, also featured bareback and saddle bronc riding, roping events, barrel racing, and steer wrestling. Women compete in throwing and hog-tying goats.

PRECEDING PAGES: A wrangler in Broken Bow readies her horses at the Little Britches Rodeo, a nationwide competition. Youngsters between eight and eighteen compete in most of the same events as at adult rodeos, though they use smaller horses and bulls.

Broken Bow has a pleasant town square with a park in its middle and a peaked and shingled bandstand in the middle of the park. I find a bench in the shade, and see in my view a Ben Franklin, Custer Floral and Gifts, Antiques, United Nebraska Bank, and Our Town Video. With an abrupt roar, a UPS truck departs Ben Franklin and stops again almost immediately at the video store. I hear a train whistle.

That night I attend the Custer County Rodeo, which is beginning a two-day run at the fairgrounds. Though still hot, there's a steady breeze in the grandstand. The American flag is first into the arena, carried by a pretty girl on a fast and fidgety horse. There are nine events: bareback riding, saddle bronc riding, calf roping, steer wrestling, team roping, bull riding, and four events for women: breakaway roping, barrel racing, steer undecorating, and goat tying. In the steer undecorating event, the object is to ride alongside a furiously fleeing steer and pluck from its back a small ribbon that has been taped there.

The bareback riders have to try to stay aboard their horses for eight seconds; half the score is for the cowboy, half for the horse, which seems fair.

The cowboys look very authentic, but I'm told by my neighbor that it's partly a pose. "If you saw them walking down the street you'd never guess they were rodeo cowboys. They'd have on their jogging pants and tennis shoes and baseball caps. To compete, they have to dress a certain way. It's a rule: You've got to wear jeans and boots and a long-sleeved shirt. And no caps. Absolutely no caps. Only cowboy hats."

When the bronc riders come out of the gate and start bouncing up and down, clouds of dust arise from the horse. The cowboy hats go flying. And when you see daylight between the bottom of the cowboy and the top of the horse, you know the horse is about to win.

Broken Bow is just on the eastern edge of the sand hills, according to my neighbor in the grandstand. "When you're driving and there are cornfields alongside the road, you're not in the sand hills," he tells me. "When the cornfields disappear, you are." The next day, heading west, huge, spindly irrigators endlessly spray cornfields but, sure enough, they soon disappear, replaced by what look like dunes with grass growing on them. Which, in fact, is pretty much what sand hills are. Blackbirds perch on swaying marsh grasses, and turkey vultures grimly circle overhead.

IN TRYON, POPULATION 100, THE seat of McPherson County, a young woman in shorts is using a weed whacker to trim the edges of the sidewalk at the courthouse. I stop at Aunt Bea's for a mid-morning snack. There's a sign in the window: "This Establishment Is a Smoking Area In Its Entirety." Four old-timers are having their morning

*Sprouting boots, fence posts run toward the horizon. Old-timers say the tradition began
with ranchers marking fences so they could find their way home in deep snow; others say that,
since boots walk a lot of miles, sentimental owners simply hate to part with them.*

coffee, and when the handsome young sheriff comes in, they engage in friendly
banter. "You better watch yourself, " one tells the sheriff. "There's an election
coming up." The sheriff is going on vacation to Colorado tomorrow, and the
old-timers want to know what to do with the bodies of intruders they shoot
during his absence. "Should we just drag 'em to the curb, or what?" one wonders. The sheriff has stopped by to get a thermos of ice water to take to his
wife—who is whacking weeds at the courthouse!

I head north from Tryon on Rt. 97, in the heart of the sand hills. A
hawk with ruffled feathers sits studying his terrain atop a utility pole, which
sits atop a hill. In one pasture, a solitary bull is lying down, his legs tucked
under him like a cat, chewing his cud, glaring at the passing traffic as if we're
keeping him awake. The highway suddenly drops down and down to cross
the Dismal River, which has quite a healthy flow; it's ten or twelve feet wide,

muddy, with high steep sand bluffs alongside it and grassy banks, where swallows dart.

I head west on Rt. 2 with railroad tracks at my right elbow, and lunch at the Double J-T Café and Bar in Hyannis, population 210. Two bicyclists, skinny men from Holland in tight black spandex, come in. "Lots of hills!" one says.

West and north of Hyannis is a memorial to someone I admire. A roadside historical marker says: MARI SANDOZ 1896-1966. The countryside here is remote and empty: no traffic, no trees, no houses, only cattle in the fields and migrating pelicans floating on the ponds. Mari was born here and is buried nearby, though she lived much of her life in the east. The sign calls her "historian, novelist, and teacher." She wrote, it continues, about "how man shaped the plains country and how it shaped him." I have the lonely place absolutely to myself. Wind ruffles the grasses and bird songs drift up from a pond. Hay bales and a barbed-wire fence are the only human indicators.

Now I'm back on Rt. 92, headed back for Tryon, having made a big circle. Patches of exposed sand look like bunkers on a golf course. Solitary men in pickups always wave with one index finger when you meet them on these little roads.

I see on my map an intriguing place: the Nebraska National Forest. What can that be like? The forest totals 141,549 acres and is in two sections, one up in the northwest corner of the state, the other—which I visit—in central Nebraska, northeast of Tryon in Thomas and Blaine Counties. A wild turkey saunters into the road as I drive upward, sees me coming, changes its mind, and saunters back. The forest is the brainchild of Dr. Charles Bessey, professor of botany at the University of Nebraska. Around the turn of the century, he envisioned a forest on treeless tracts of sand hills and created a nursery here to produce seedlings for what's termed the "country's largest man-made forest." Since 1926 the nursery has supplied seedlings to state and tribal forestry programs in Kansas, Nebraska, and South Dakota and to national forests in the Rocky Mountain region. The nursery covers 50 acres and each year produces 3.5 million bareroot conifer and hardwood seedlings of 50 different species. I see them in their beds, being sprinkled by sprayers, all in neat rows, thousands of baby trees an inch tall.

Verdant after a rainy spring, the sand hills stretch parklike across Nebraska's Panhandle. Many highways here run for hundreds of miles through such sparsely settled land.

FOLLOWING PAGES: *Aged ruts recall the days of the pioneers as they reach toward an arcing double rainbow, perhaps a suitable symbol of the pot of gold the immigrants sought.*

I WORK MY WAY FARTHER NORTH toward Valentine. Nebraska has had a wet spring, and the sand hills reflect it, sprouting several shades of delicate green. They undulate gently, and roll with a natural rhythm.

A fort, one of a string of military posts throughout Nebraska, established in the last century to keep the peace in Indian country, once sat on the Niobrara River four miles from Valentine. Its soldiers had a peaceful life, fighting no battles, putting down no uprisings. It was shut down in 1912, the same year Mr. J. W. Gilbert of Friend, Nebraska, offered 6 buffalo, 17 elk, and several deer to the federal government if land could be found for them. Fort Niobrara was chosen, and in 1936 a small herd of Texas longhorn cattle was added. Now the Fort Niobrara National Wildlife Refuge encompasses about 30 square miles and is home to some 400 buffalo, 60 elk, and 275 longhorns.

An auto route takes you among the animals. The bison look like parked boulders on a distant hillside, and the longhorns make me glad I'm safely in my car. Those horns! Those malevolent glares! The animals are grazing on bluestem and switchgrass. Prairie dogs wag their tails like puppies and scurry for their holes when I drive by.

The signboard pointing the way to Fort Falls has been used by the buffalo as a rubbing post and looks like they've been chewing on it. I follow its arrow to the falls, park, and descend to the base. It's cool and ferny at the bottom, and I follow a rough trail alongside the stream to where it empties into the Niobrara. *Backpacker* magazine has named the Niobrara among the top ten canoeing rivers in the U.S., and indeed it looks inviting: slow and gentle and shaded. It begins life as a small trout stream in Wyoming and flows into the Missouri River about 130 miles east of Valentine.

My first destination in Valentine is the Snake River Hat Company on Main Street. A few years ago Ron Hollenbeck, who was born in Nebraska, gave up a career in sales and real estate to move to Valentine and begin making cowboy hats. "I was 47 years old before I figured out what I wanted to be when I grew up," he says. "This is very rewarding. I get to make something that's not only functional but also beautiful."

In the last six years he figures he has made about a thousand hats, which he sells for 200 or 300 dollars each. Beautiful examples of his work are displayed around his shop. Nearly all the equipment he uses is antique, in use for 150 years. Old wooden crown blocks in various sizes and shapes sit like skulls on a sort of lazy Susan. He buys beaver felt from Winchester, Tennessee. "I buy 'em just like this—a bonnet-shaped piece of felt. Most of the beaver are imported, I guess, and where they originate I wouldn't know."

Cowboy hats curl up on the sides in a jaunty fashion and down at the

Mist rises along the Niobrara River, northern Nebraska's major stream.
Rising in eastern Wyoming, it joins the Missouri near Yankton, South Dakota.
A portion of its length is protected in the Wild and Scenic River System.

front and back, in a more serious fashion. "I can usually tell by a guy's age what kind of hat he's gonna want," Ron tells me. "Young guys all want black hats. In the early 1900s, only the villains wore black hats. Now they all want to look like bronc riders. They're extremely fussy. And vain. They'll stand in front of that mirror and look and look. Older fellows who come in, nine out of ten, won't order a black hat."

Ron walks me through the various steps involved in making a hat, though, as he says, hat makers are a secretive lot. "I had to learn on my own. The attitude is, if you want to learn, figure it out for yourself." There's a steamer, a sander, an iron, a sewing machine. There's even a tool called a "puller-downer." He uses an ingenious implement to produce a diagram of the shape of my head and an intricate one to get its size. He seems impressed that I'm a seven-and-five-eighths, the same as JFK.

As I'm leaving, one of those "older fellows" comes in. He says to Ron, "I've decided, I'd like to have one good hat before I die."

Valentine, as you might expect, has one very busy day each year when it mails thousands of cards and letters with its postmark prominently displayed. The weekend of my visit it was throwing another sort of party—a city-wide

garage sale. Nearly 60 participating residences have been listed in the paper, each given a sentence or two to list the items for sale. Number 12, for instance, on Sunshine Greenhouse Road, has "blinds, typewriter, prom dresses, flower tubs, clothing, all sizes, knickknacks, yard windmill."

Out early to beat the crowds and the heat, I find the shoppers cheerful and eager to buy; everyone says good morning. As I stroll up and down the shady streets, I find lots of baby clothes, mismatched mugs and cups, boxes of romance novels, exercise equipment, artificial flowers, and used clothing piled on tables and hanging forlornly on hangers. And more exercise equipment. On one lawn, a young woman is sitting patiently waiting for customers with a gleaming motorcycle parked just behind her. "Yours?" someone asks. "No, but everybody wants to buy it," she says. Nearby, someone's dog is being driven frantic by all the strangers walking up and down its street.

In the end, I buy just two things: a Dale Carnegie paperback called *How to Stop Worrying and Start Living*, for a dime, and a two-inch-by-five-inch wooden wall hanging; it has two red-and-green daisylike flowers painted on it, and a message: "If friends were flowers I'd pick you." When I get home, I give it to a friend, who looks at me sideways.

WEST OF VALENTINE, RT. 20 RUNS along the lower edge of South Dakota on its way to Wyoming. It passes through Cody and Merriman and Clinton and Hay Springs, through sand hills and plains, and just south of the Pine Ridge Indian Reservation.

Chadron, the county seat of Dawes County, population 5,588, calls itself "the city of no strangers." It's in the midst of its Fur Trade Days celebration when I arrive. Early trappers brought their furs to several trading posts in the region, including the Bordeaux Trading Post just outside of Chadron, where the town's Museum of the Fur Trade now stands. Traders used the nearby White River as a highway to the Missouri.

Three days of events are planned, from an art show and Lions Club barbecue, to a liar's contest, a parade, a carnival, a pancake breakfast, a volleyball tournament, and a street dance. Not to *(continued on page 154)*

In costume, vacationers join a wagon train to retrace a part of Nebraska's Oregon Trail. An immigrant woman in 1851 wrote, "People who do come…must not be worried or frightened at trifles. A lazy person should never think of going to Oregon."

FOLLOWING PAGES: *Seemingly ablaze, a coal train passing through wetlands and marshland in the sand hills catches the last light of evening.*

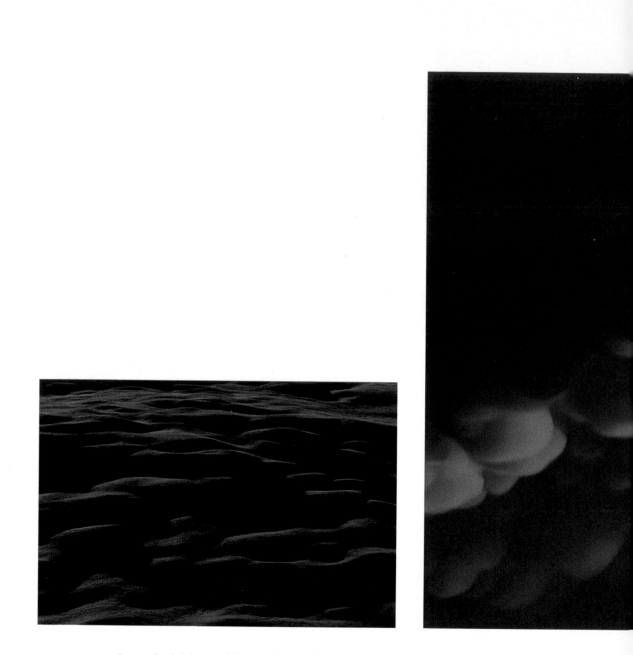

Lumpy clouds (above, right) mimic bumpy hills, as sky mirrors sand hills. Writer Willa Cather, who grew up in this part of Nebraska, wrote of the weather and the harsh land and the struggles of the pioneers to tame it. She got much material from old immigrant women, she said. "I used to think them underrated, and wanted to explain them to their neighbors. Their stories used to go round and round in my head at night."

mention music, a regatta, and fireworks. I have a buffalo burger in Court-house Square, with potato salad and lemonade, and sit in the shade to listen to the Turtle Creek Bluegrass Band perform. They play "I'll Take Love Over Lonesome." Benches are made of bales of straw with 2x12s resting on them.

After lunch I wander by the art show and the craft show and the carnival, which is pretty quiet at midday. I check out what's billed as the World Famous Championship Buffalo Chip Throw on Main Street. Throwers are competing for gold, silver, and bronze buffalo chip plaques in three divisions: men, women, and children. Some of the chips look suspiciously like the cow patties from my Iowa youth, but never mind. Some contestants throw over-hand, some side arm, some Frisbee style, some underhand, some backhand. Some of the chips fly apart in fragments. One toss goes awry and sails into the stands, scattering the judges. I have some homemade ice cream at the Con-gregational Church.

There's another rodeo at the fairgrounds that night. I watch in amaze-ment as Casey McGooden does a virtually perfect somersault over the head of his horse during the saddle bronc ride.

Westward I go, into the far upper corner of Nebraska, past Fort Robinson, another fort built to keep the peace. It was here that Crazy Horse, one of the most enigmatic yet seminal of the Indian leaders, was killed on September 5, 1877, dying of a bayonet wound on the floor of the adjutant's office. According to writer Larry McMurtry, notable was "…the terrible, pitiable, Lear-like grief of Crazy Horse's parents: they wandered the fort for three days, sobbing, wailing, rending their garments, refusing all succor." They buried their son somewhere in the area, but no one knows exactly where.

During World War II, the fort served as a training site for more than 3,000 dogs, used in the war in sentry duty, trail and attack work, message bear-ing, and mine detection.

North of the fort is the bizarre Toadstool Park, a strangely sculpted land-scape eroded from ancient volcanic ash and flood deposits. In the parking lot there's a van full of a family and dog from Colorado, and another family with children camped at one of the campsites. It's very hot and quiet; I don't even hear any bird songs. Pronghorn stand up to their bellies in the tall grass along-side the parking lot, and beyond them I walk through a herd of a hundred or so cattle, who turn to watch me as I walk by. They're mesmerized; it's as if they've never seen a human.

A narrow, sandy trail runs among the toadstools, along streambeds, through gullies, and over sandstone rocks. The region was given its fanciful name by its first visitors in the late 1800s. The trail is carefully marked and

"Going, going, gone," cries auctioneer Lon Lemmon at an estate sale near Chadron.
Lon and his wife Carolyn have been in the auction business in this part of Nebraska for more
than 40 years. Here they help a widow dispose of the belongings from 56 years of marriage.

easy to follow, for it looks like it would be possible to wander off and get lost.

Thirty million years ago miniature horses, humpless camels, gigantic tortoises, pigs, and even rhinoceroses roamed here. Now only bits of their bones and tracks remain.

An hour south of Fort Robinson is an American oddity I've long wanted to see: Carhenge. About 40 American automobiles from the '50s and '60s have been painted boulder gray and arranged—some with their trunks buried in the ground, others atop one another like lintels—in the same configuration as Stonehenge in England. Paul Phaneuf, the president of Friends of Carhenge, shows me around. "It was the idea of a local fella named Jim Reinders," says Paul. "He was a petroleum engineer who was in England during the days of the North Sea oil exploration and saw Stonehenge there. When Jim's father died, his family wanted to erect a monument to him, and this is what they came up with. A replica of Stonehenge, but made with cars."

"It's not an idea that would have occurred to everybody," I venture.

"No no no. In fact, people said to him, what on Earth are you doing. The Nebraska Department of Roads got involved, said, hey, this is a junkyard;

*Cool oasis on a summer night, Zesto feeds the sweet tooth of Alliance, seat of Box
Butte County. Says the Chamber of Commerce, "We're just a small, quiet community with
a lot of friendly people." A large railroad maintenance shop employs many.*

remove it or screen it. Fortunately the arts community said, this guy's a genius.
This is art. It was dedicated on June 21—the summer solstice—of 1987.

"Friends of Carhenge erected the Heel Stone, a big old Cadillac, in 1991.
We attached ropes to the front of the car, long ropes 120 feet long, and on the
signal about 750 people started pulling. That car fell right into its pit, straight
up." Mostly the community of Alliance supports Carhenge, though, as Paul
says, "we have to be very careful to disassociate ourselves completely from the
Druids."

Flowering clover surrounds Carhenge today, and nodding wheat grass.
Paul says, "I wonder what archaeologists will think a thousand years from now."

On the far western edge of the sand hills, Scotts Bluff rises out of the grasslands like the prow of a huge ship. Immigrants passing through on their way
west were happy to see this major landmark, for it meant their journey was
one-fourth finished. It offered a welcome relief from the seemingly endless trek
across the prairie. The bluff is a national monument now, and I ride up in a
park service shuttle bus, scrunched up against a little Hispanic girl. From the
top, I can see for miles in every direction and hear the mournful hoot of trains
down in the valleys.

Spookily reminiscent of Stonehenge in England, Carhenge rises on the prairie near Alliance. Though a nearly exact replica of Stonehenge, this construction fails to act as the same sort of celestial calendar, due to its more southerly latitude.

During my visit to Nebraska, the state launches its first scenic byway, along the North Platte Valley from Scottsbluff to Ogallala, a distance of about 125 miles. I set out to drive it, retracing the route of the Oregon and the Mormon Trails, but backward.

The drive begins inauspiciously as four lanes lined with Super 8s and car dealerships and four tall round towers pressed up against one another like cigars in a box; Western Sugar is painted on the side. The highway soon narrows to two lanes with a yellow line down the middle and the inevitable railroad track and utility line on my right, all of us heading east. The industrial suburbs drop away, and I'm in farmland with irrigators spraying a delicate mist onto fields. A railroad crossing arm comes down just as I reach it, lights blink, and a train with its whistle sounding goes rolling by. As I sit quietly waiting, the ground shakes gently beneath me.

Leaving Melbeta, I come to the first of the round scenic byway signs: red, white, and blue, with a bird, a windmill, and a road. Looming up in the distance is what looks like an inverted funnel: Chimney Rock, rising several hundred feet above the surrounding plain. In 1841 traveler Rufus B. Sage wrote: "Oct. 26…soon afterward arrived opposite the 'Chimney,' *(continued on page 162)*

157

Stone mushrooms sprout in Toadstool Geologic Park near Crawford (opposite). Erosion and ancient lava flows combine here to create a wonderland of bizarre shapes and mazes (above).

FOLLOWING PAGES: *Like the smokestack it's named for, Chimney Rock reaches some 500 feet above the prairie; immigrants on the Oregon Trail could spot it from 30 miles away.*

an extraordinary natural curiosity that had continued in view and excited our admiration for some four days past…a grand and imposing spectacle, truly;—a wonderful display of the eccentricity of Nature!" Rufus was among the waves of migrants that came through here, some on the Oregon Trail, others with the Mormons, still others heading to California for the 1849 gold rush. Probably 400,000 people traveled along this route, mostly by covered wagon. It was often a crowded trail; some reported seeing wagons all the way to the horizon day after day. A good day would take the travelers ten miles; a slow day maybe four.

About 4,000 Mormons spent the winter of 1846 camped on the Nebraska shore of the Missouri River. In the spring of 1847, the first group, known as the Mormon Pioneers and led by Brigham Young, left camp and headed west. They followed the north bank of the North Platte River and passed Chimney Rock on May 26, 1847. One of them devised an odometer by tying a red cloth to a wagon wheel and counting the revolutions.

I pause in Bridgeport for a sundae at Hardees, then miss the turnoff for a couple more geologic landmarks: Courthouse Rock and Jail Rock. Still on Rt. 92, I cross Pumpkin Creek on a narrow blacktop, too new to have a yellow line, and pass one of those big irrigators that has been parked too close to the highway; it hurls a gallon of water onto my windshield—*splat!*—and scares me half to death.

At Broadwater the river is thick and muddy and almost in flood. I gain on, catch up with, and pass a coal train without exceeding 60 mph. The hamlet of Lisco, too small to have a population listed, slows me down to 50 with a speed limit sign. The Lisco Superette is OPEN. The highway is suddenly thick with huge green machinery, wheat harvesters moving to another field. They lumber along like something from *Star Wars*, on gigantic black wheels.

Oshkosh, population 986, also has a Superette, as well as a Texaco station and the Shady Rest Motel. There are some terrific big trees, but in less than a minute I'm back in the countryside.

NEAR ASH HOLLOW I STOP TO READ a historic marker. It tells of the battle of Blue Water on September 3, 1855, when the U.S. Army defeated an encampment of Indians, killing 86 warriors and capturing many women and children. "This first yet often overlooked military campaign against the Lakota kept the Overland Trail open but only postponed until 1863-4 a war between the two nations."

At the visitor center of the Ash Hollow State Historical Park, the flag snaps and crackles in a hot wind. Inside are displays of memorabilia and artifacts of the battle. "I never saw a more beautiful thing in my life," wrote the correspondent from the *Missouri Republican,* who was at the slaughter. Mannequins

A barn kitten gets a kiss from Bonnie Simonson, who ranches with her husband Joe in the heart of the sand hills. The third generation of her family to live in the sand hills, Bonnie grew up 70 miles from any town. "There were just trail roads, so a trip to town took all day." Today weak cattle prices cause worries, but Bonnie loves the sand hills "for the peacefulness. At night, all you hear is silence—unless the coyotes are howling."

are dressed in uniforms of the times. A private in the 6th Infantry is about to shoot his ear off, it appears. Another soldier, a private in the 2nd Dragoons, is wearing a cap that's too small. It makes him look a little tipsy.

I end my visit at Lake McConaughy, just north of Ogallala, though it's a place the pioneers wouldn't have seen. It's Nebraska's largest reservoir; locals call it Big Mac and fish for walleye on its 35,700 surface acres. I stop at the office and am welcomed by a jolly woman. "Have you got a map of the area?" I ask. "I'm a stranger here."

"Well not for long," she says, shaking my hand. "Hi. I'm Cindy."

Cindy points me toward the best places for seeing plovers and terns and bald eagles, and I find a lakeshore picnic table where I sit and have a banana. Wakes of powerboats make a gentle slapping noise on the sandy beach, and from the distance come the shrieks of teenage girls learning to water ski.

I think, maybe that's another nice thing about back roads and byways: You can't be a stranger for very long. I'll test this premise one more time, in the far northwest corner of the country, on the drizzly Olympic Peninsula. ∎

ROADS OF COAST AND FOREST

Olympic Peninsula

SOME OF THIS COUN-
try's most magnificent coastline defines the western
edge of the Olympic Peninsula. From Cape Flattery
in the north to Grays Harbor in the south, sea stacks
and sandy beaches and rocky coves and forested
bluffs line the byways. Sea lions sprawl on rocky
islets, as seabirds soar overhead.

The *Silver Duchess,* Capt. Dennis Moss com-
manding, edges away from the wharf in downtown
Westport, Washington, and turns her stubby nose out
toward the choppy waters of Grays Harbor.
A couple of sea lions bawl like cattle and follow along,
hoping for a handout. *Hula Girl* is just ahead of us,
an unlikely name for a boat on this cold, blustery, rainy
day. We pass a green buoy, swaying in the swell, with
a sea lion lounging on it. He looks cold and wet and
miserable, and I think: I'm glad I'm not a sea lion.

We're looking for the gray whales that are migrating from their breeding grounds in Baja California to the Bering and Chukchi Seas, where they feed through the summer on tiny crustaceans and mollusks. They were hunted nearly to extinction in the not-too-distant past but now are plentiful. In fact, scientists think, there are about 22,000 of them, about the same as before hunting began.

Besides the captain and his deckhand, Jim, we are four—myself and three other tourists, two women and a man. When Captain Moss turns *Silver Duchess* into the wind it's bitterly cold, and we hunker down within our windbreakers. One of the women stands at the bow, her hands clasping the railing, like the heroine in *Titanic*.

Once into the middle of the large harbor—an inlet, really—we immediately begin seeing whales. They often appear first as a cloud of mist on the horizon. We shout and point and the captain turns toward the sighting. The whales' mottled black backs emerge from the water and a cloud of mist rises from their blowholes. We *ooh* and *ahh* like fireworks spectators. A whale not far away sticks its head straight up out of the water, like a periscope. Its mouth is agape and we can see its baleen. It appears to be looking around. "He's what we call 'spyhopping,'" says the captain. "You wonder who's watching who." Two whales surface near enough for us to see the barnacles around their heads. "An adult male averages about 42 feet long," says the captain, "and the female is slightly larger. They weigh about 45 tons."

There are rules governing the captain's actions here. He cannot get within a certain distance of the whales without shutting down his engine. He points us toward the place where a whale has been spotted and we glide closer. Occasionally, they appear right at our gunwale. It's a thrill to see them. Camera shutters click furiously.

We spend a couple of hours chasing gray whales, then—with spray hitting the cabin windows—head back to the wharf, past a big sign painted at dockside: Please Tip Your Deckhand. We dutifully obey and disperse.

THE SPANISH AND THE BRITISH visited and claimed the Olympic coast for their countries in the 1770s, but Hoh and Quileute Indians repelled settlement. A Britisher, John Meares, named Mount Olympus in 1788. A few years later, British Capt. George Vancouver explored the Puget Sound region, and an American, Robert Gray, charted the mouth of the Columbia River. He also gave his name to the harbor where today the gray whales visit.

The 6,400-square-mile peninsula is bounded on the west by the Pacific, on the north by the Strait of Juan de Fuca, and on the east by Hood Canal and Puget Sound. Its interior is largely given over to *(continued on page 174)*

*Twilight tints a rocky coast at Ruby Beach near Kalaloch. Coastal Highway 101 skirts
this beach, passing sea stacks and pillars carved as surf gnaws away coast.*

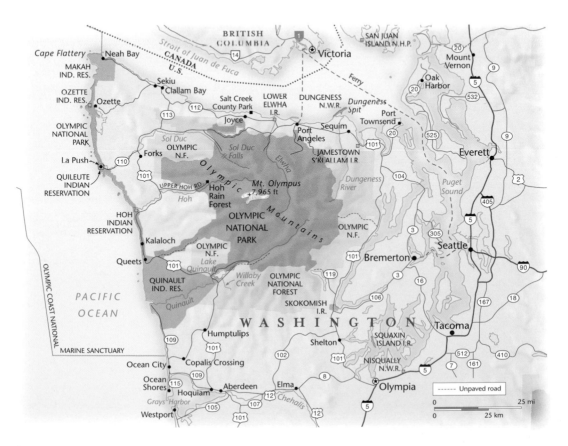

Sunset blasts through a hole in the rocks near La Push, a Quileute native community.
Above, tide and light trace rhythmic patterns in sand and mud on coastal flats.

FOLLOWING PAGES: *Sea stacks clutter offshore waters of the Olympic Coast National*
Marine Sanctuary; it encompasses some 3,310 square miles, supports rich fishing
and shellfishing grounds, and is visited by 29 species of whales, dolphins, otters, and porpoises.

Both anchor and canopy, bull kelp flourishes along the Olympic coast. Thick forests of the plants can reach up more than 60 feet from the seafloor, giving homes to fish and resting areas for seabirds. Kelp also absorbs some impact of waves, reducing beach erosion.

the Olympic Mountains, part of the Coast Ranges, and Olympic National Park. The Seattle Press Exploring Expedition blazed a north-south crossing of the Olympics, via the Elwha River Valley, in the winter of 1889-90.

The coastal lowlands are a quilt of private and public lands, including eight Indian reservations. The park, named both a World Heritage Site and an International Biosphere Reserve by the United Nations, contains one of the best and largest examples of undisturbed temperate rain forest in the western hemisphere, the largest intact stand of coniferous forest in the contiguous 48 states, and the largest wild herd of Roosevelt elk.

Olympic National Forest flanks the park on three sides; when first set aside by President Cleveland in 1897, it preserved more than two million acres but has been reduced in size since then.

A huge area of shores, beaches, offshore islands, kelp forests, reefs, shoals, and underwater canyons are protected by the Olympic Coast National Marine

Sanctuary. Partly because of the peninsula's position halfway between the boreal north and the temperate south, and partly because of the combination of river mouths, coves, sand and gravel beaches, and mild year-round climate and nutrient-rich offshore waters, the sea here has tremendous natural diversity.

The western side of the peninsula is the wettest place in the contiguous U.S., with some areas getting drenched by an average of 167 inches of rain a year. The ecosystem of the Olympics is pretty well intact, except for one missing element: the endangered gray wolf, which preys on elk and deer. There's a move to reintroduce the animals to the peninsula, a popular idea to some but a controversial one to others. There are some habitat-dependent species— salmon in the rivers, heathers in the high country, mollusks in the tidal flats, northern spotted owls in the old-growth forests, Roosevelt elk in the rain forests—that biologists monitor to judge the health of the overall habitat. Logging, fishing, pollution, hunting, introduced species, recreational use, population growth, and encroaching development all impact the peninsula ecosystems.

I'M MAKING A SORT OF CLOCKWISE tour around the Olympic Peninsula, a fertile ground for back roads and byways. I make a start the morning after the whale-watching trip by finding a Westport café with 30 or so pickups overflowing the parking lot and strung alongside the street. Inside, middle-aged men, mostly fishermen, are doing what such men regularly do at breakfast: complaining.

"Goddam herring," I hear one say.

"I wonder who's buying all those boats?"

"The banks."

"How you gonna compete with subsidized boats."

"This is my wedding anniversary," one man tells the waitress.

"No kidding. Congratulations."

"I've been married for 23 years and haven't seen her for 12."

"Oh."

Another man nearby tells his companions of a pet raven he once had that tried to land on a ceiling fan. "Those feathers were *flying!*"

Heading north on Rt. 109, I find the ocean crowded with resort clutter: Best Westerns and McDonalds, Anchor Savings Bank, go-carts and bumper cars. Ocean City's beach is busy with pony rides and kids and dogs chasing sea gulls. An impressive surf is rolling in and people are bundled up in the cold. Kites soar overhead. There's a steady roar from the surf. Some of the big fluffy clouds have ominous-looking gray bottoms. There are seagulls the size of turkeys.

Heading inland, blue-and-white highway signs have a painting of a big wave rolling in, and say "Tsunami Evacuation Route." Going cross-country

Their traditional slim dugout canoes rigged with outboard motors, Quileute Indians race across a placid lagoon. Since ancient times, coastal Native Americans like the Quileute have enjoyed the rich bounty of the forest and the sea.

toward Humptulips, a road sign says "Elk Crossing." Holsteins populate cattle farms. Copalis Crossing has a Texaco station and a couple of stop signs. Its post office looks like a one-room schoolhouse, complete with flag. I'm still on the Tsunami Evacuation Route, I see. Every hillside has been heavily logged a number of times; young, replanted trees of every size grow alongside the road in neat patches. Sprinkles drop occasionally from those gray-bottomed clouds.

U.S. 101, running north near the coast, curves inward to bypass most of the Quinault Indian Reservation and touches the tip of Lake Quinault. The lake is six square miles and 250 feet deep in places. Trumpeter swans frequently winter here.

I stroll for a bit on a short interpretive nature trail through the rain forest near the lake. Ferns and mosses are shiny with wet, and Willaby Creek, roaring and white, comes tumbling down out of the hills. Like all the streams on the peninsula, it doesn't have far to go to get from its source to the sea. The four most common rain forest conifers around me, according to a signboard, are western hemlock, Douglas-fir, western red cedar, and Sitka spruce. A little hill makes me puff, and I pause to listen to an unseen songbird high in the trees. "Windblown trees account for over 80 percent of the death of trees in

By the sea, bikers and beachcombers share the sand at Ocean Shores, a 6,000-acre peninsula at the mouth of Grays Harbor, one of the major seaports on the Pacific Coast. Miles of sandy beaches extend north from here.

the Olympic rain forest," another sign tells me. "Old age, disease, and fire make up the rest." In the last 100 years, ten known hurricane-force storms have battered the northwest coast, blowing down millions of trees in the Olympic rain forest. I look up at the canopy, as a signboard directs me to do, and see droplets of water falling toward me, almost in slow motion, like a 3-D movie.

A rough road, single lane, bumpy with potholes and ruts, circles Lake Quinault, up and down hills, around corners. An elk startles me by suddenly stepping out of the underbrush, then meandering off. It's bigger than a deer, but smaller than a moose; more graceful than a moose, but less graceful than a deer. Its coat is two or three shades of brown.

Most of the wooded mountains you see on the Olympic Peninsula outside the national park show evidence of logging, especially clear-cutting, a controversial and ugly system that foresters insist is the most economical and practical method of harvesting timber. The little town of Forks sits in the heart of logging country, and heavy timber trucks come barreling down the roads, trailing clouds of shredded bark and twigs. The town's Timber Museum, on the highway, displays artifacts chronicling the history, economy, and culture of logging, along with historic photographs and old logging equipment. *(continued on page 182)*

Moss-covered boulders steer a tumbling stream in Olympic National Park (opposite).
The park's rain forests are among the wettest places in the U.S., some receiving an average of
167 inches a year. Some of it drops in a gossamer veil at Sol Duc Falls (above).

FOLLOWING PAGES: *In a riot of growth, the Hoh Rain Forest blankets the western section*
of the park. Sitka spruce dominates in this western-facing, temperate valley.

Sawdust flies when chain-saw artist Dennis Chastain of Forks goes to work. Eleven years ago his wife asked the former mill and logging worker to carve her a mushroom. He tried it, and, as he jokes, "business just mushroomed."

The town's newspaper, the *Forks Forum,* keeps citizens abreast of goings-on and visitors entertained with the weekly police reports. On one day in March, for instance, police responded to these complaints:

"A vehicle was stuck in the mud on Merchant Rd.

"A go-cart was reported racing up and down the street on Lupine Ave., subjects were contacted and advised.

"The front door was open at a vacant house on Bogachiel Way.

"Balloons were causing a traffic hazard by the transit center on Forks Ave."

And the next day, "Intoxicated female was asked to leave the bar at the Vagabond as she was giving customers and bartender verbal hardship; female was driving a blue jeep."

I follow one of those thundering logging trucks to its destination—the Allen Logging Company, which offers, according to its employees' business cards, "logs, veneer, chips and studs." Mike Simmons, log buyer and jack-of-all-trades, shows me around. In hard hats, we prowl through the buildings, where giant machinery growls and thunders and reduces logs to manageable elements. On metal steps and walkways we thread narrow passageways with machinery screaming at our elbows. Men look up from their work as we pass, but only for a moment, for the conveyors never stop.

"We harvest mostly western hemlock," shouts Mike. "Second-growth trees that are 40 to 45 years old." In the yard, crows are hopping and hovering over the logs, finding bugs. "Each truck that arrives here carries a load of 26 tons." A huge yellow machine with claws picks up the entire load with one bite. "About 30 loads a day arrive here, so we're producing up to 100,000 feet of lumber a day." Gleaming saw blades whirl too fast to watch and make short work of the logs. Conveyors carry chips one direction, rejected logs another, and finished boards a third. A skid of 2x4s has "A HD 4 96" stenciled on its end. Mike explains: "The 'A' is for Allen, this company. 'H' means hemlock and 'D' dried. The '4' stands for April, and '96' means the 2x4s are 96 inches long."

He gives me a list of about 50 items made from wood, from aerospace shields to wallpapers, from apparel fabrics to vacuum-cleaner bags, from toothbrush handles to fishing lures.

F ROM FORKS I MAKE AN EXCURsion into Olympic National Park, backtracking on Highway 101, then turning east on the Upper Hoh Road to the Hoh Rain Forest. A late-season dusting of snow has transformed the roadsides and the conifers, draping them with white frosting.

Trees 1,000 years old and 300 feet tall survive here. Spruce, hemlock, and fir make a solid canopy overhead; vine and bigleaf maple, red alder, and sorrel tangle in the understory, and mosses, lichens, and ferns sprout everywhere in the soggy forest. As I set off from the visitor center, several big elk stand up out of the snow where they've been spending the night.

It's early in the day, and the forest is very quiet. Now and then a clump of snow falls from above, making a sodden splat; dribbles patter on my parka hood. Little birds flitting through the undergrowth offer fluty songs. A wooden bridge carries me across a gurgling stream, its bed bright with green grasses and mosses. Beards of spike moss dangling from the trees overhead look like the Spanish moss of the South. All the vegetation looks shiny and clean, as if it's just been washed. I hear the Hoh River before I come to it, and its rocky bed is ten times wider than the small braided stream that's running down it. Driftwood, washed white, is piled like pick-up sticks.

The Hoh Rain Forest's signboards are better written than those of many parks. One near the river speaks of "the clattering of cobbles" in the river. Another, titled "Decor of the Rainforest," says, "Here youth and age are entwined. Shelf fungus fruits on a dying spruce trunk, a colonnade of trees straddles a decaying nurse log. Your senses detect the unique atmosphere of the rainforest: wind in the upper story barely rippling the lower floor; air plants growing green upon green; or subtler features like the light filtering from treetops down through tapestries of moss."

After my walk I stop at the Hard Rain Café for lunch. "I'm a little hungry," I tell the woman proprietor. "Well, we've got a little menu," she says, indicating a blackboard on the wall behind her. I opt for a chicken-breast-and-ham sandwich and onion rings. An elderly local woman, a crusty rancher, is talking with the proprietor. She claims to have seen two of her cows chasing a cougar across her pasture recently. "Their tails were up and they were *movin'!*" When the subject of reintroducing wolves to the peninsula comes up, she snorts and says, "Put 'em on the Indian reservations."

As it happens, an Indian reservation is my next stop. The Makah Nation inhabits the farthest tip of the farthest corner of the peninsula. A nation of whale and seal hunters, the Makah have had a thriving civilization here on the coast for thousands of years. A complex ritual life assured safety and success in the hunt; bountiful resources from both land and sea assured a rich material culture. Back then, the Makah lived in a string of coastal villages; one of them—Ozette—was partially buried by a huge mud slide several hundred years ago. Archaeologists recovered some 55,000 artifacts from the site, which are now displayed and stored in the Makah Museum in the village of Neah Bay. It's regarded as one of the finest small museums in the country, and I'm eager to see it.

The drive to Neah Bay is another beauty: the Strait of Juan de Fuca on my right, forested mountains on my left. Rocky beaches are washed by a gentle surf, and scraggly trees stand just back from them. In one, a bald eagle sits, staring out over the strait.

Neah Bay is a collection of wooden structures clustered behind an impressive new marina. There is a large supermarket with a deli, a pizza place or two, a gas station, a T-shirt shop, a motel, and a couple of RV hookups. The town seems like the absolute end of the road, but it has its own website and two espresso stands. A small but tidy cemetery on the edge of town has graves marked by Christian headstones and American flags as well as by brightly painted totem poles with the familiar motifs of northwestern coastal Indian art.

The museum is a handsome, slate-gray, low-slung building. Its director, Janine Bowechop, is conducting a staff meeting when I arrive, and, though the museum hasn't yet opened for the day, I'm offered the opportunity to stroll through the dim galleries alone. There are dioramas illustrating marine and forest environments; a full-size longhouse—a replica of the sort the Makah built years ago; a couple of beautiful cedar canoes, hollowed from huge logs. There are artifacts from whaling and sealing, from hunting and fishing, from

Through the fog, mountains of Olympic National Park rise beyond the Quinault River.
At least 15 short rivers drop from highlands to lowlands on the peninsula. Early settlers and
pioneers used this one as a route to the interior.

FOLLOWING PAGES: *Three Parker sisters—from left, Theresa, J., and Doris—along with*
Philip, Doris's grandson, gather at J.'s home in Neah Bay to weave baskets, a family
as well as a Makah Indian tradition. "Philip is the fourth generation," says Theresa.
She adds, "We always have children with us when we weave or when we gather materials—
western red cedar, bear grass, sedge, seaweed, roots. It's important to teach them the proper ways
of gathering to keep our natural resources sustainable."

woodworking and plant gathering. Other displays illustrate games of the Makah, their basketry, and their spinning.

Staff meeting over, Janine welcomes me into her office. She looks very young to be the director of such an important museum. A Makah herself, she attended elementary school here in Neah Bay, junior high and high school in Tacoma, and college in New England. She got a degree in cultural anthropology. "But I don't consider myself an archaeologist." She began working in the museum in 1991 and became executive director in 1995.

She was too young to take part in the archaeological dig at Ozette, "but we certainly made a lot of school or family trips there when I was a kid. It was an exciting time for us as children, though I probably didn't *(continued on page 190)*

Where the road ends: Cape Flattery—the tip of the tip—stubs its rocky toe on the Pacific Ocean at the far northwestern corner of the peninsula (above). Light diffused by towering trees (above, left) bathes the narrow, winding road to the cape. Gray whales pass close by here, and seabirds nest where the Makah have hunted and fished for centuries.

Hoping for a handout, gulls flock to the Neah Bay dock, where Zacarias Espinoza cleans fish. Halibut was a staple for the ancient Makahs, and salmon came seasonally to rivers and streams. Herring and smelt were caught just off sandy beaches, the smelt in fine-mesh dip nets and the herring on the points of rakes.

really realize until I was a teenager how special it was—that every tribe in the country didn't have an incredible excavation and wasn't building a beautiful museum to house the artifacts." She was involved as a replicator as a child, weaving some of the mats that are in the canoes, for instance, as an 11- or 12-year-old.

"There's a lot of goodness and beauty here in Neah Bay," she says. "I don't mean we're flourishing, but the economy is strong. And there are wonderful things about this area. An Indian anthropologist once said that the Makah Reservation is the most beautiful land on the continent that still belongs to Indians."

I ask whether living at the end of the road is a good thing for the people, or a bad thing. "This is not the end of the road," she laughs. "It's the beginning. We don't have the violent crime here that you get in urban areas, but a lot of disruptive influences still get to us. You can get a hundred channels on your TV here just as well as anywhere. But there's a lot to be said for living far from large populations. We've maintained a lot of values that are very specific to the Makah people, partly through our isolation. Kids here dress as hip as kids anywhere, but they still know what it means to take care of their grandparents the way the Makah are supposed to."

She's proud of the museum's connection with the community. "We give tours for school groups and elders, arrange demonstrations of arts and crafts, and sponsor lectures. We're developing a botanical garden where we'll grow the plants that were used by our ancestors for tools, medicines, things like that. Community members will be able to come here and actually harvest plants they want to use."

The population of Neah Bay is slowly growing, Janine tells me. "We just brought in a few new members in an adoption process. That is, if you're less than one-quarter Makah by blood you have to be accepted in a formal process by the tribe. The enrollment of the tribe is a little over 2,300 now. That's pretty close to precontact numbers."

I HEAD BACK ALONG THE SHORE OF the strait, through Sekiu and Clallam Bay and Joyce, to Port Angeles, the largest town on this part of the peninsula. Nice restaurants are available here, as well as a place to walk off over-indulgences: Ediz Hook, a naturally formed sand spit, juts into the strait and curves around to form Port Angeles's deepwater harbor. It's a popular spot for walkers and joggers and dog walkers. Cormorants perch on logs, looking like funerary urns, and harlequin ducks bob on the swell. Gulls pass overhead, yelling as if the sky were falling.

At Salt Creek County Park west of town I can smell the smoke from campers' fires at the campground. Fort Hayden, built here in the early 1940s, protected the entrance to Puget Sound during World War II; the guns are gone now, made obsolete by airplanes and more powerful guns on ships, according to a sign, but the camouflaged batteries survive. On Tongue Point, looking toward Canada, I watch as freighters and tankers move slowly by. Little birds—I think they're scoters—paddle through the surf, sometimes riding over it, other times diving headfirst into it, like surfers. They emerge shaking their heads, again like surfers. A young man and woman from Scandinavia sit patiently at water's edge, with a pair of binoculars, watching for whales.

Charming little Port Townsend lies about 50 miles east of Port Angeles. It boasts the best examples of Victorian architecture north of San Francisco, with more than 70 buildings on the National Register of Historic Places. Most of the buildings are from the mid-19th century, and many in the historic downtown area are now shops, galleries, and restaurants. I have lunch in one of them and listen as a woman at the next table, sipping a martini, tells her companion, "I was too busy growing up myself to be a good parent." I shop until my two-hour parking limit is up, then move my car and shop some more. In mid-afternoon I have an ice cream cone down by the waterfront, and the seagulls, screamers and bullies that they are, nearly take it away from me.

Between Ports Townsend and Angeles the Dungeness Spit reaches for 5.5 miles into the strait. It may be the nation's largest natural sand spit. The lighthouse near its tip, built in 1857 and automated in 1976, is the oldest north of the Columbia River. The spit is prime walking territory, with the strait on the left and a quiet bay on the right. Undisturbed eelgrass beds attract feeding Pacific black brant.

A signboard at the spit's trailhead tells me I may see 44 different birds—from cormorants and white-winged scoters to dowitchers and yellow legs. The spit makes a long graceful curve before me, punctuated at its end by the lighthouse, which looks, even through my binoculars, a very long way away. Foamy white surf is beating against the left side. The spit is narrow—just a few yards—and driftwood polished to a soft gray is piled helter-skelter down its center. The wind off the ocean is chilly. I walk and walk, then come to a discouraging sign that says I've gone half a mile. Several bald eagles take turns cruising down the length of the spit, just a few feet overhead, scavenging for refuse. One glares down at me with a look that seems to say: "Live Free or Die." It flies tilted slightly into the breeze, so it looks as if its flying catercornered.

Behind me on the shore the huge, snow-covered Olympic Mountains stretch from horizon to horizon, like a Cinemascope movie. I decide it's not important to make it all the way to the lighthouse; after all, it's not only 5.5 miles to the thing, it's 5.5 miles back. Returning, I meet three elderly ladies, jolly and pink-cheeked, tightly zippered into their Gortex parkas. They've come about half a mile and want to know if they're about there yet. They tell me they've seen several scoters and a loon.

IN NEARBY SEQUIM—PRONOUNCED "squim"—I lunch on chowder and a halibut sandwich, because it's halibut season. Sequim sits in the rain shadow of the mountains and receives just an average of 17 inches of rainfall a year. Farming here would be impossible without irrigation, which was introduced toward the turn of the century. The surveyor who helped settlers divert water from the Dungeness River accepted potatoes from the next season's crop as part of his wages. When water successfully flowed, on May 1, 1896, jubilant farmers celebrated, and Sequim has staged an Irrigation Festival each year since.

While I eat, I browse in the *Sequim Gazette* and learn of a program intended to reduce collisions between elk and vehicles on Highway 101. For 75,000 dollars, officials plan to outfit eight-to-ten lead animals in the Sequim herd with signal-emitting transmitter collars. When the elk get within one-eighth of a mile of the highway, the signals will trigger flashing signs along the roadway, warning motorists.

Workers harvest a bountiful crop on the Purple Haze Lavender Farm near Sequim.
"You can smell it a mile away," says owner Mike Reichner of the farm.
Tucked into a rain shadow behind the Olympics, the region has an arid climate ideal for
growing lavender. Used in aromatherapy, in perfume, and as an herb in cooking,
versatile lavender is "the Swiss Army knife of herbs," says Mike's wife Jadyne.

FOLLOWING PAGES: *Rugged Olympic Range rises from sunset-pink clouds; only the less*
traveled roads touch such places, chief reward of America's back roads and byways.

I had planned to complete the circle around the peninsula on that same Highway 101 but am foiled by mud slides. A wet spring has sent tons of mud sliding down onto the highway on the eastern edge of the circle, closing the highway. But I find my way to Bremerton and study a ferry schedule. To the people of Puget Sound, these ferries are as ordinary as buses, but to an outsider they can be intimidating. So, apprehensive, I arrive at the ferry terminal a full two hours too early. A kindly ticket seller lets me leave my car and sends me off to explore the nearby antique shops.

But soon I'm boarded with other passengers on the ferry *Kitsap,* my car safely parked below and a cup of hot coffee in my hand. With a sudden mournful hoot—which makes men flinch and children cry—*Kitsap* slides away from her slip. Seattle and its airport—and home—are just around the corner. ∎

INDEX

NOTES ON CONTRIBUTORS

RON FISHER was a staff writer and editor in the Society's Book Division for 30 years before retiring in 1994. He lives in Arlington, Virginia, and contributes occasionally to Society publications. His volume *America A.D. 1000: The Land and the Legends,* the story of life in North America at the end of the first millennium, appeared in 1999.

SARAH LEEN has been a freelance photographer for the National Geographic Society since her college internship in 1979. She has been a regular contributor to NATIONAL GEOGRAPHIC magazine having published ten stories, ranging from Russia's Kamchatka peninsula to Amelia Earhart. Her most recent story covered the Mexican volcano Popocatepetl. Leen has also contributed to several Geographic books including *Great Journeys of the World.* She lives in Edgewater, Maryland, with her husband Bill Marr.

ACKNOWLEDGMENTS

The Book Division and the writer and photographer of this book would like to thank the following people: Charlie Acuff, Beth Alexander, Tony Angelle, Katie Austin, Mervin Baras, Gladys Beamish, Victoria Cooper, Danny Brown, Gregg Bruff, Paul Cox, Mary Ethel Emanuel, Rick Fuller, Greg Girard, Charles Hammond, Ron Hitchcock, Neil Houk, Dan and Laurie Houle, Gordon Howard, Jay Huner, Kolleen Irvine, Dean Knudsen, Robin Lambert, Casey Landreneau, Dell Le Fevre, Karen Lemmon, Lorene Lewis, Jim Mason, Riley Mitchell, Larry Mowrey, Tom Nemacheck, Dave Ochsenbauer, Dean Osborne, Chris Pease, Gayle Pollock, Donnie Richardson, Jerry Schumacher, Sterven Seven, Michael Smithson, Bob Steelquist, Polly Taylor, Steve and Bevin Taylor, Cliff Thevenin, Clark Thorsen, Paul Wannarka, Delores Wasserburger, Craig Winnie, Michael "Tunaboy" Woodhouse, and Ted Wyrick.

America's Back Roads and Byways

By Ron Fisher
Photographs by Sarah Leen

Published by the National Geographic Society

John M. Fahey, Jr. *President and Chief Executive Officer*

Gilbert M. Grosvenor *Chairman of the Board*

Nina D. Hoffman *Senior Vice President*

Prepared by the Book Division

William R. Gray *Vice President and Director*

Charles Kogod *Assistant Director*

Barbara A. Payne *Editorial Director and Managing Editor*

David Griffin *Design Director*

Staff for this Book

Rebecca Lescaze *Editor*

David Griffin *Art Director*

Marilyn Moffard Gibbons *Illustrations Editor*

Diana Vanek *Researcher*

Carl Mehler *Director of Maps*

Mapping Specialists, Ltd., Joseph F. Ochlak, Michelle H. Picard *Map Research and Production*

R. Gary Colbert *Production Director*

Lewis R. Bassford *Production Project Manager*

Richard Wain *Production Manager*

Meredith C. Wilcox *Illustrations Assistant*

Peggy J. Candore *Assistant to the Director*

Dale-Marie Herring *Staff Assistant*

Elisabeth MacRae-Bobynskyj *Indexer*

Manufacturing and Quality Management

George V. White *Director*

John T. Dunn *Associate Director*

Vincent P. Ryan, Gregory Storer *Managers*

Phillip L. Schlosser *Financial Analyst*

The world's largest nonprofit scientific and educational organization, the National Geographic Society was founded in 1888 "for the increase and diffusion of geographic knowledge." Since then it has supported scientific exploration and spread information to its more than nine million members worldwide.

The National Geographic Society educates and inspires millions every day through magazines, books, television programs, videos, maps and atlases, research grants, the National Geography Bee, teacher workshops, and innovative classroom materials.

The Society is supported through membership dues and income from the sale of its educational products. Members receive NATIONAL GEOGRAPHIC magazine—the Society's official journal—discounts on Society products, and other benefits.

For more information about the National Geographic Society and its educational programs and publications, please call 1-800-NGS-LINE (647-5463), or write to the following address:

National Geographic Society
1145 17th Street N.W.
Washington, D.C. 20036-4688
U.S.A.

Visit the Society's Web site at www.nationalgeographic.com.

Library of Congress Cataloging-in-Publication Data

Fisher, Ron,
   America's back roads and byways / Ron Fisher ; photographs by Sarah Leen.
      p.   cm.
   Includes index.
   ISBN 0-7922-7860-7
   1. United States--Description and travel. 2. United States--Pictorial Works. 3. Roads--United States--Pictorial works. 4. Scenic byways--United States--Pictorial works. I. Leen, Sarah. II. Title.

E.169.04 .F565 2000
973.92--dc21   99-088107
                                                      CIP